Manuela Burkhardt
Dorothea Neumann

Cozy Country
Knits

Socks, Hats, Jackets and Sweaters
with Classic Rural Charm

TRAFALGAR SQUARE
North Pomfret, Vermont

First published in the United States of America in 2013 by

Trafalgar Square Books

North Pomfret, Vermont 05053

www.trafalgarbooks.com

Originally published in German as *Ländlich gestrickt*

Copyright © 2012 frechverlag GmbH, 70499 Stuttgart, Germany (www.frechverlag.de)

English language translation © 2013 Trafalgar Square Books

This edition is published by arrangement with Claudia Böhme Rights & Literary Agency, Hannover, Germany (www.agency-boehme.com).

ISBN: 978-1-57076-624-4

Library of Congress Control Number: 2012952548

MODELS: Manuela Burkhardt (pp. 18-21, 40-42, 66 - 84), Lana Grossa Studio (p. 8-17, 22-24, 28-39, 43-45, 48-53); Dorothea Neumann (pp. 25-27, 46/47, 54-65)

PHOTOS: frechverlag GmbH, 70499 Stuttgart, light spot, Michael Rudder, Stuttgart (cover, pp. 66/67, 93); Patrick Brinkschulte Stuttgart (p. 54-65), photo studio Ullrich & Co., Renningen (pp. 86-92, 94/95); fotolia (pp. 8, 10, 11, 38 photo crew (p.13), PoetConcepts (p. 15), Fotodil (p 19, 21) Mellimage (pp. 23, 24), imageteam (p. 26) aquaria-girl1970 (pp. 29, 31), koya79 (pp. 35, 36), Alexandr Vlassyuk (pp. 41, 42), Swetlana Wall (pp. 44, 83), daseaford (p. 47), felinda (p 49), Irina Fischer (pp. 52/53), unpict (p. 57), cmnaumann (p.59), INFINITY (p. 61), vadim yerofeyev (p. 63), pizuttipics (p.65), Birgit Reitz-Hofmann (p. 69), Nik (p. 72), Elnur (p. 75), Eric Isselée (p. 77), gtranquillity (p. 77), P. 79 Christian Jung; point of light, Jochen Frank, Laichingen (remaining photos)

PRODUCT MANAGEMENT: Eva Barbara Hentschel, Miriam Heil

EDITORIAL: Cosima Kroll, Bönnigheim

LAYOUT: electrolytes, Petra Schmidt, Munich

DESIGN: Petra Theilfarth

TRANSLATION FROM GERMAN: Donna Druchunas and Carol Huebscher Rhoades

We thank Lana Grossa GmbH, Gaimersheim, for assistance in the preparation of this book.

Printed in China

10 9 8 7 6 5 4 3 2 1

Table of Contents

Foreword

Life in the country awakens many pleasant associations in us: the clocks tick quietly as we slow down in a hectic world, enjoying our own private island of tranquility. On long walks, we listen to the sounds of birds and the murmur of small streams and feel very close to nature. The fresh air clears my head and allows my mind to rest, and a return home brings the aroma of freshly baked, homemade bread.

All of this is also found in *Cozy Country Knits*—as the soft and fluffy wool and tweed yarn slips through your fingers with each stitch that you make, you'll feel the comforting seclusion of country life. Classic shapes with timeless cables and pattern stitches make the projects enjoyable both to knit and wear.

Whether you choose cozy jackets, casual sweaters, chic hats or practical accessories, the rural charm will captivate you!

Warmth for Any Weather

Lofty and warm yarns make these garments perfect for a walk in town or a short hike in the woods when you need some fresh air. The casual styles invite you to snuggle up in front of the fire for a stay-at-home weekend.

Sideways Cabled Jacket

The unusual knitting direction gives the classic ribbed cable knit a totally new and sophisticated look.

LEVEL OF DIFFICULTY
Intermediate

SIZES
S (M) / European 36/38 (40/42)
The numbers for the smaller size are listed first and those for the larger size are within parentheses. When only one number is given, it applies to both sizes.

MATERIALS
Yarn: (CYCA #4), Lana Grossa Alta Moda Alpaca (90% alpaca, 5% virgin wool, 5% polyamide; 153 yd/140 m / 50 g), Green 23, 700 (750) g
Needles: U.S. sizes 9, 10, and 10½ / 5.5, 6, and 6.5 mm: 32 in / 80 cm circular needles or sizes needed to obtain gauge.
Cable needle
Stitch markers
Crochet hook: U.S. size J-10 / 6 mm

GAUGE
22 sts and 25 rows in Cable Rib pattern using U.S. 10 (6 mm) needles = 4 x 4 in / 10 x 10 cm when slightly stretched.

PATTERN STITCHES
K2, P2 Ribbing
Row 1 (RS): (K2, p2) across; if 2 sts rem at end of row, end k2.
Row 2: Knit the knits and purl the purls.

Cable Rib Pattern
Only RS rows are shown on the chart. On WS rows, knit the knits and purl the purls as stitches face you. The repeat is 32 sts and 36 rows.

Garter Selvages
Slip the first stitch of every row knitwise and knit the last stitch of every row for the selvage (edge sts). Stitch counts include the edge sts.

⊟ = K on RS, P on WS

◼ = P on RS, K on WS

⬛⬛⬛/⬜⬜⬜ = Sl 3 sts to cn and hold in back, k3, k3 from cn

⬛⬛⬛\⬜⬜⬜ = Sl 3 sts to cn and hold in front, k3, k3 from cn

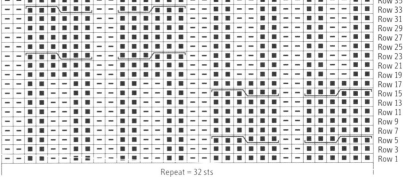

Row 35
Row 33
Row 31
Row 29
Row 27
Row 25
Row 23
Row 21
Row 19
Row 17
Row 15
Row 13
Row 11
Row 9
Row 7
Row 5
Row 3
Row 1

Repeat = 32 sts

INSTRUCTIONS

The body of the sweater is worked from side to side. The arrow in the schematic shows the direction of knitting.

LEFT FRONT

Beg at the front edge, with U.S. 10 / 6 mm needle, CO 148 (150) sts.

Row 1 (RS, beg at bottom edge and end at neck edge): Sl 1 knitwise (selvage), work in k2, p2 ribbing to last st (for S end with k2, for size L end with p2), k1 (selvedge).

Neck shaping

Continue to work in k2, p2 ribbing with selvages as established, and *at the same time*, on the 15th row, inc 1 st at the neck edge, then inc at the neck edge every other row 6 times. Next, CO 2 sts at neck edge once, CO 3 sts at neck edge 3 times, then CO 4 sts at neck edge once. Work all incs into k2, p2 ribbing—170 (172) sts.

When piece measures 6 in (15 cm) and 38 rows are completed, end after working a WS row.

Next row (RS, begin at bottom edge): Sl 1 (selvage), work 4 sts in k2, p2 ribbing as est, pm, work the next 160 sts in Cable Rib pattern (= 5 patt rep across), pm, work the next 4 (6) sts in ribbing as est, end k1 (selvage).

Shoulder

Work even in patts as est with cable patt between markers for 5 (6) in / 13 (15) cm and 32 (38) rows from beginning of cable patt.

Armhole shaping

BO 46 (48) sts at beg of the next row. Work even until armhole measures 2 in / 5 cm and 12 rows have been completed, then CO 46 (48) sts and resume working in patts as est before armhole shaping.

RIGHT FRONT

Work as for Left Front, beg at front edge and reversing shaping.

BACK

Beg at the right side seam, CO 124 sts with U.S. 10 / 6 mm ndl.

Beg at the bottom edge, set up patts as foll:

Row 1 (RS): Sl 1 (selvage), k2, p2, work the next 118 sts following Cable Rib chart, working the full rep 3 times and then the first 22 sts of the chart once more, k1 (selvage).

Note: Begin at Row 3 and work Rows 3 and 4 once (4 times), then continue with Row 5.

Shape Armhole

When piece measures 2 in / 5 cm and 14 rows are complete, shape armhole as follows:

Next row (RS): CO 46 (48) sts—170 (172) sts, work in patts as est to end of row. Work existing sts in patts as est and new sts in patt to match front as follows:

Next row (WS, begin at bottom edge): Sl 1, work 4 sts in ribbing as est, pm, work the next 160 sts in Cable Rib, pm, work the next 4 (6) sts in k2, p2 ribbing as est, k1.

Center Back

Work even in patts as est until piece measures 18 (19½) in / 46 (50) cm [= 113 (125) rows] from 1st armhole. End after working a RS row.

Shape Armhole

Next row (WS): BO 46 (48) sts. When the armhole measures 2 in / 5 cm and 14 rows have been completed, work Rows 35 and 36 once (4 times)—piece measures 22 (23¾) in / 56 (60) cm and a total of 142 (154) rows have been worked.

BO loosely in patt.

SLEEVES

With U.S. 10 / 6 mm needle, CO 66 sts and begin working in k2, p2 ribbing with garter edge sts.

When piece measures 6 in / 15 cm and 38 rows have been completed, inc 1 st at each side of next row, then every 8th row 10 (4) times, and every 6th row 3 (11) times, working all incs into ribbing—94 (98) sts.

When piece measures 15¾ in / 40 cm and 100 rows have been worked after the first inc, mark the beg and end of the row. Work even for 14 rows = 2 in / 5 cm. BO.

FINISHING

Wash and dry flat to block.
Sew shoulder seams.
With U.S. 9 / 5.5 mm ndl and WS facing, pick up and knit about 140 sts around neck opening.

Row 1 (RS): K1 (edge st), work in k2, p2 ribbing to last 3 sts, k2, k1 (edge st).

When collar measures 2 in / 5 cm, change to U.S. 10 / 6 mm needles, then, when collar measures 4 in / 10 cm, change to U.S. 10½ / 6.5 mm needles. When collar measures a total of 10¼ in / 26 cm, BO loosely in patt.

Sew sleeve seams from cuff to markers. Sew side seams. Set sleeves into armholes and turn up cuffs.

Work 1 row of single crochet around the bottom edge of the jacket, making sure that your crochet tension matches that of the knitting so the edge does not pull in or flare out.

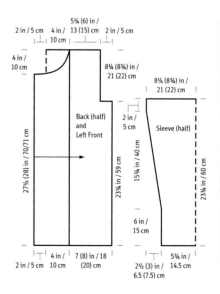

Casual Elegance

This jacket is an exercise in opposites: all at the same time, it is incredibly cozy and casual yet feminine and elegant.

LEVEL OF DIFFICULTY
Easy

SIZES
S (M, L) / European 36/38 (40/42, 44/46)
The numbers for the smallest size are listed first and those for the larger sizes are within parentheses. When only one number is given, it applies to all sizes.

MATERIALS
Yarn: (CYCA #4), Lana Grossa Niente (40% Merino wool, 30% alpaca, 28% polyamide, 2% spandex; 114 yd/104 m / 25g) in Light Rust 01, 350 (400, 450) g
Needles: U.S. size 8 / 5 mm: 24 in / 60 cm circular or size needed to obtain gauge
Stitch markers

GAUGE
20 sts and 26 rows in St st = 4 x 4 in / 10 x 10 cm

Schematic: see page 96.

PATTERN STITCHES
Stockinette Stitch (St st)
Knit RS rows and purl WS rows.

Chain Selvage
Knit the first st of the row through the back loop and slip the last stitch pwise wyif. Edge sts are included in the stitch counts.

INSTRUCTIONS
Fronts and back are worked together in one piece. The arrow in the schematic (see page 96) shows the direction of knitting.

FRONTS AND BACK
Left Front
CO 162 sts and work in St st (with chain selvage at each side) for 15 (15½, 15¾) in / 38 (39, 40) cm and 100 (102, 104) rows have been worked.

Left Armhole
Next row (RS): K85 sts, BO 32 sts, knit rem 45 sts.
Working back and forth on these 45 sts, BO 2 sts at armhole edge twice, then CO 2 sts at armhole edge twice.
Return to the 85 sts and, working back and forth, BO 2 sts at armhole edge twice, then CO 2 sts at armhole edge twice.
On the next row CO 32 sts over armhole opening—162 sts.

Back
Work even in St st over all sts until piece measures 14 (15, 15¾) in / 36 (38, 40) cm and 94 (100, 104) rows have been worked after left armhole.

Right Armhole and Front
Work as for left armhole. Work even until right front measures the same as left front. BO loosely kwise on RS.

SLEEVES
CO 82 sts and work in St st (with chain selvage at each side).
Dec 1 st inside edge st at each side on the 9th (9th, 31st) row, then every 6th (12th, 30th) row 9 (5, 1) times—62 (70, 78) sts rem.
When sleeve measures 11 (12¾, 13¾) in / 28 (32, 35) cm and 74 (84, 92) rows have been worked, attach a marker at each side of the row.

Shape Sleeve Cap
Dec 1 st inside edge st at each side of next row then every other row 15 (10, 6) times. BO rem 30 (48, 64) sts loosely.

FINISHING
Wash, pin to measurements, and dry flat to block.
Sew sleeve seams to markers.
Mark the center of each sleeve cap and sew sleeves into armholes.

Cozy Sampler Stitch Jacket

Worked on big needles, this jacket is a quick-knit that can be ready for your next walk! The interesting mix of patterns will keep the knitter engaged.

LEVEL OF DIFFICULTY
Intermediate

SIZES
S (M, L) / European 36/38 (40/42, 44/46) The numbers for the smallest size are listed first and those for the larger sizes are within parentheses. When only one number is given, it applies to all sizes.

MATERIALS
Yarn: (CYCA #6), Lana Grossa Alta Moda Kid (60% mohair, 40% virgin wool; 65 yd / 60 m / 50 g), Amaranth Heather 02, 1050 (1100, 1150) g
Needles: U.S. size 13 / 9 mm: 32 in / 80 cm circular or size needed to obtain gauge
3 matching buttons, approx 1¾ in / 4.4 cm in diameter

GAUGE
11.5 sts and 17 rows in Reverse St st = 4 x 4 in / 10 x 10 cm
8.5 sts and 25 rows in Brioche Moss st = 4 x 4 in / 10 x 10 cm
12.5 sts and 17 rows in Moss st = 4 x 4 in / 10 x 10 cm
8.5 sts and 25 rows in Brioche Rib = 4 x 4 in / 10 x 10 cm

PATTERN STITCHES

Garter Selvage
Knit the first and last stitch of every row for selvage (edge st). Edge sts are included in the stitch counts.

Moss Stitch
Row 1 (RS): (K1, p1) across.
Rows 2 & 4: Knit the knits and purl the purls as sts face you.
Row 3: (P1, k1) across)
Rep Rows 1-4 for pattern.

Reverse Stockinette Stitch (Rev St st)
Purl RS rows; knit WS rows.

Stockinette Stitch (St st)
Knit RS rows; purl WS rows.

Brioche Moss
Charted patt is worked back and forth in rows. The repeat is 2 sts and 4 rows.
Stitches are shown as they are worked, and both RS and WS rows are shown on the chart. Read the RS rows from right to left and the WS rows from left to right. Begin the row with the stitch before the repeat, work the 2-stitch repeat across, and end the row with the 2 stitches after the repeat. Repeat Rows 1-4 for pattern.

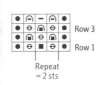

Row 3
Row 1
Repeat = 2 sts

● = Selvage
⊖ = Yo, sl 1 pwise
■ = Knit
⋒ = K2tog (yo and slipped st)
⋒ = P2tog (yo and slipped st)
— = Purl

Brioche Rib

Charted patt is worked back and forth in rows. The rep is 2 sts and 4 rows. Stitches are shown as they are worked, and both RS and WS rows are shown on the chart. Read the RS rows from right to left and the WS rows from left to right. Begin the row with the stitch before the repeat, work the 2-stitch repeat across, and end the row with the 2 stitches after the repeat. Work Rows 1-4 once, then repeat Rows 3 and 4 for pattern.

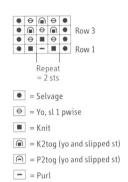

Repeat
= 2 sts

- ⊙ = Selvage
- ⊖ = Yo, sl 1 pwise
- ■ = Knit
- ⌂ = K2tog (yo and slipped st)
- ⌂ = P2tog (yo and slipped st)
- − = Purl

Full-Fashion Decreases:

At the beginning of the row, after the 3 selvage sts, k3tog (2 sts decreased); at the end of the row, before the 3 selvage sts, work dec as sl 1 kwise, k2tog, psso (2 sts decreased).

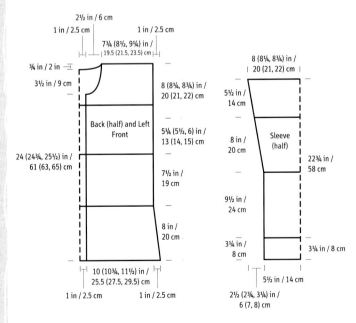

2½ in / 6 cm

1 in / 2.5 cm   1 in / 2.5 cm

7¾ (8½, 9¼) in /
19.5 (21.5, 23.5) cm

¾ in / 2 in

3½ in / 9 cm

8 (8¼, 8¾) in /
20 (21, 22) cm

Back (half) and Left
Front

5¼ (5½, 6) in /
13 (14, 15) cm

24 (24¾, 25½) in /
61 (63, 65) cm

7½ in /
19 cm

8 in /
20 cm

10 (10¾, 11½) in /
25.5 (27.5, 29.5) cm

1 in / 2.5 cm   1 in / 2.5 cm

8 (8¼, 8¾) in /
20 (21, 22) cm

5½ in /
14 cm

8 in /
20 cm

Sleeve
(half)

22¾ in /
58 cm

9½ in /
24 cm

3¼ in /
8 cm

3¼ in / 8 cm

5½ in / 14 cm

2½ (2¾, 3¼) in /
6 (7, 8) cm

INSTRUCTIONS

Note: Because each pattern stitch works up to a different gauge, be sure to increase or decrease between patterns as explained in the instructions.

BACK

CO 55 (57, 61) sts. Beg working Brioche Moss.

When piece measures 8 in / 20 cm and 50 rows have been worked, on the next row, inc 18 (20, 22) sts evenly across and beg working Moss st—73 (77, 83) sts.

Armhole shaping

When 32 rows of Moss st have been worked and Moss st section measures 7½ in / 19 cm, on the next row dec 8 (6, 8) sts evenly across and beg working Rev St st—65 (71, 75) sts.

When Rev St st measures 5¼ (5½, 6) in / 13 (14, 15) cm and 22 (24, 26) rows of Rev St st have been worked, place markers at the beg and end of the row to mark the beg of the armholes.

When armhole measures 2 (2¼, 2¾) in / 5 (6, 7) cm and 8 (10, 12) rows have been worked after markers, on the next row, dec 16 (18, 18) sts evenly across and beg working Brioche Rib for the yoke—49 (53, 57) sts.

Neck shaping

When Brioche Rib section measures 5¼ in / 13 cm and 32 rows of Brioche Rib have been worked, BO the center 7 sts for the neck and work each side separately.

On the next RS row and then on every other row, dec 2 sts using Full-Fashion Decrease at the neck edge twice. When the neck measures ¾ in / 2 cm and 6 rows have been worked, BO the rem 17 (19, 21) shoulder sts. Re-attach yarn on opposite side of neck edge, and rep for the second shoulder, reversing shaping.

LEFT FRONT

CO 25 (27, 29) sts and work in pattern as for the back, marking armhole position when same length as back. Inc and dec as follows:

When changing from Brioche to Moss st, inc 10 sts—35 (37, 39) sts.
When changing from Moss st to Rev St st, dec 3 sts—32 (34, 36) sts.
When changing from Rev St st to Brioche Rib, dec 9 sts—23 (25, 27) sts.

Neck shaping

When Brioche Rib section measures 1½ in / 4 cm and 10 rows of Brioche Rib have been worked, BO 4 sts at the neck edge once, then dec 2 sts using Full-Fashion Decrease at neck edge once. BO rem sts when piece measures same as back to shoulder.

RIGHT FRONT

Work as for left front, reversing shaping.

SLEEVES

CO 25 sts. Work in Brioche Rib.

When sleeve measures 3 in / 8 cm and 20 rows have been completed, begin working Brioche Moss.

When Brioche Moss section measures 9½ in / 24 cm and 60 rows of Brioche Moss have been worked, on the next row inc 12 sts evenly across and beg working Moss Stitch—37 sts.

Inc 1 st at each side of the following 7th (3rd, 7th) row, then every 8th (8th, 6th) row 5 (6, 7) times, working all incs into Moss Stitch patt—49 (51, 53) sts.

When Moss Stitch section measures 8 in / 20 cm and 34 rows of Moss Stitch have been worked, change to St st

Work even for 5½ in / 14 cm, then BO loosely kwise on RS.

FINISHING

Wash pieces, pin to measurements, and dry flat to block.

Sew the side seams up to the armhole markers.

Sew the sleeve seams, working the first 3 in / 8 cm of the cuff seam on the outside, so, when you fold up the cuff, the seam is hidden.

Button Band

CO 7 sts and work in Brioche Rib until piece measures 24 (24¾, 25½) in / 61 / 63, 65 cm. BO in patt.

Buttonhole Band

Work as for button band, making 3 buttonholes as foll: For the 1st buttonhole, after 9 in / 23 cm: BO 2 sts in the center of the band and CO 2 sts over the gap on the next row. Work 2 more buttonholes spaced 4¼ in / 11 cm apart.

Sew the bands to the front edges of the sweater.

Collar

With RS facing, pick up and knit 49 sts around neck edge.

Row 1 (WS): K1 (selvage), work in k1, p1 ribbing to last st, k1 (selvage).

Work in Brioche Rib until piece measures 5¼ in / 13.5 cm and 34 rows have been worked.

Dec 2 sts using Full-Fashion Decreases at beg and end of of next row, work 3 rows even, then rep from * to *—41 sts rem.

BO all sts loosely in patt.

Sew in sleeves and sew on buttons.

Traditional Gansey Sweater

This chic sweater takes the traditional English fisherman sweater into the twenty-first century, making it quite fashionable again.

LEVEL OF DIFFICULTY
Advanced

SIZE
M / European 38/40

MATERIALS
Yarn: (CYCA #5), Lana Grossa Bingo Melange (100% Merino wool, 88 yd/80 m / 50g), Olive 72, 1100 g
Needles: U.S. size 8 / 5 mm: two 32 in / 80 cm circulars or size needed to obtain gauge
Crochet hook: U.S. size G-6 (4.0 mm)
Cable needle

GAUGE
17 sts and 25 rows in St st = 4 x 4 in / 10 x 10 cm

TECHNIQUES
Channel Island CO
Pull out a tail of yarn approx twice as long as you need for casting on. Double the yarn by folding it in half.

Make a slip knot with both strands of yarn, approx 6 in (12 cm) from the end of the double tail. Hold the tail in your left hand and the single yarn attached to the ball in your right hand.

*YO with the single yarn. While holding the yo in place with your right hand, take the double tail in your left hand and wrap it counter-clockwise around your thumb, twice.
Insert the right needle underneath both strands around your thumb (the single strand yo is still in front of the needle). Take the single strand, and wrap it around the needle as if you were knitting the stitch and pull tightly—2 sts made. Rep from * alternating between yo and k sts, until the desired number of sts CO.

PATTERN STITCHES
Garter stitch
Back and forth: knit all rows.
In the round: *knit 1 rnd, purl 1 rnd and rep from *.

Stockinette Stitch (St st)
In the round: knit all rounds.

INSTRUCTIONS
The sweater is knit up to the armholes in the round in the manner of traditional English fisherman sweaters (Ganseys). After inserting underarm gussets, the front and back are separated and the upper body is worked back and forth. The shoulder seams are closed with three-needle bind-off and the collar band is knit. Finally, the sleeves are knit down from the armholes to the cuffs in the round.

Charts A, B1, B2, and C

Charts are worked in the round or back and forth, as indicated in the pattern. The stitches are shown as worked. When working in the round, read all chart rows from right to left. When working back and forth, read RS rows from right to left and WS rows from left to right.

Chart A

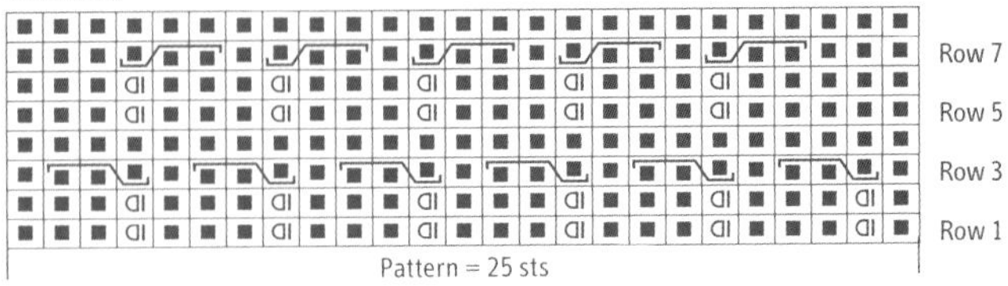

Pattern = 25 sts

Row 7
Row 5
Row 3
Row 1

Chart B1

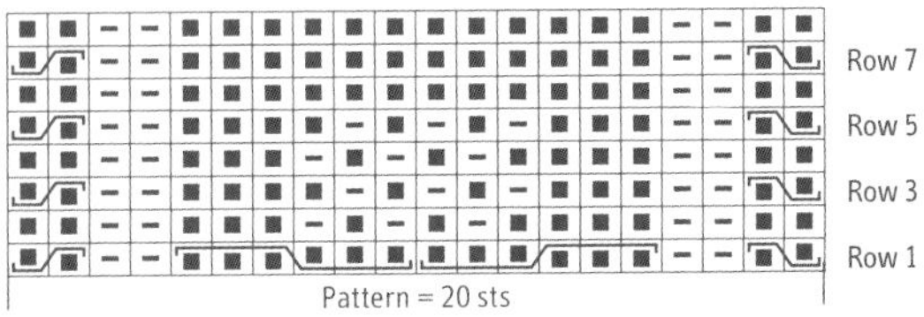

Pattern = 20 sts

Row 7
Row 5
Row 3
Row 1

Chart B2

Pattern = 20 sts

Row 7
Row 5
Row 3
Row 1

Legend:

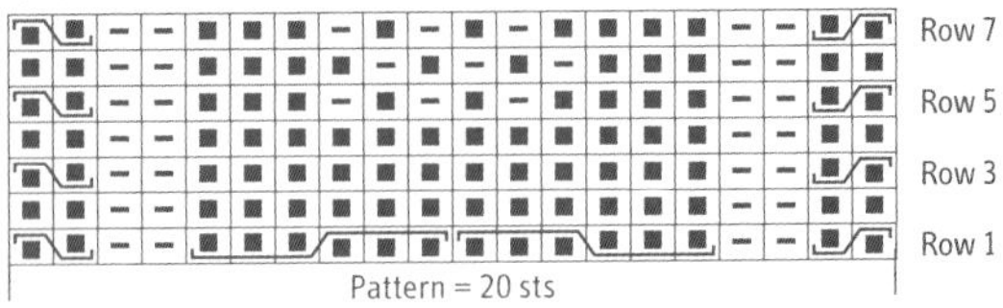

- ■ = Knit
- − = Purl
- ☐ = No stitch
- = Sl 2 sts to cn and hold in back, k1, k2 from cn
- = Sl 1 st to cn and hold in front, k2, k1 from cn
- ◨ = Sl 1 st purlwise wyib
- = Sl 1 st to cn and hold in back, k1, k1 from cn
- = Sl 1 st to cn and hold in front, k1, k1 from cn
- = Sl 3 sts to cn and hold in front, k3, k3 from cn
- = Sl 3 sts to cn and hold in back, k3, k3 from cn
- ◆ = K1tbl
- = Sl 1 st to cn and hold in front, k1tbl, k1tbl from cn
- = Sl 1 st to cn and hold in back, k1tbl, k1tbl from c
- = Sl 1 st to cn and hold in front, p1, k1tbl from cn
- = Sl 1 st to cn and hold in back, k1tbl, p1 from cn
- = Sl 1 st to cn and hold in front, k1, k1tbl from cn

Chart C

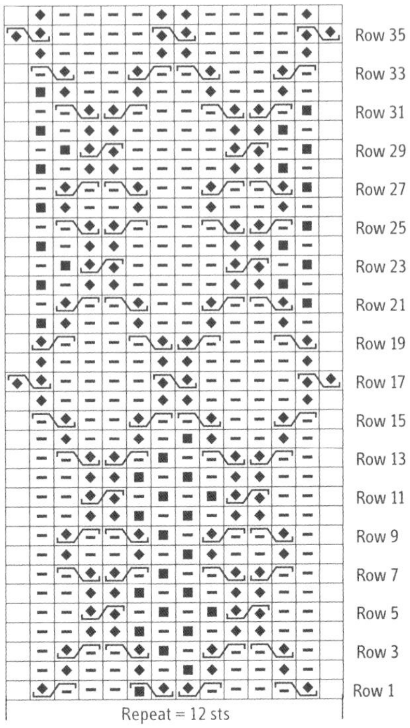

Row 35
Row 33
Row 31
Row 29
Row 27
Row 25
Row 23
Row 21
Row 19
Row 17
Row 15
Row 13
Row 11
Row 9
Row 7
Row 5
Row 3
Row 1

Repeat = 12 sts

BODY

Use the Channel Island Cast-On and CO 192 sts. Join to work in the round, being careful not to twist sts, and work 20 rnds in garter st.

In the next rnd inc 62 sts evenly around—254 sts.

Set up patts as follows: *p1, work chart A over the next 25 sts, chart B1 over the next 20 sts, chart C over the next 36 sts (3 repeats), chart B1 over the next 20 sts, chart A over the next 25 sts; rep from * once more. The two purls form faux side seams.

Repeat all rows of chart C twice, then work Rows 1-18 once more.

Shape sleeve gussets

Next rnd: *P1, M1p, work in patts as est to next side seam stitch, place marker, M1p; rep from * once more. Each gusset now has 3 sts, including the original center purl. Work 2 rnds even, then, in the next rnd M1p at the beg and end of each gusset. Increase the same way every 3rd rnd until the gusset is a total of 13 sts wide. Work 2 rnds even.

DIVIDE FOR FRONT AND BACK

Next rnd: *Work 126 sts in patt to the first gusset for back, then put the next 13 sts on scrap yarn or a stitch holder; rep from * once more for front and put front sts on a spare needle.

BACK

Work the Back sts back and forth in rows, knitting the first st of every row for a selvage, until piece measures 7½ in /19 cm from the division.

Shape neck

On row 21 of the 5th repeat of Chart C, BO the center 20 sts. Then, with 2 balls of yarn work each side separately. On every other row, BO 6 sts at the neck edge once, then BO 4 sts at the neck

edge once. When piece measures 26¼ in (67 cm), place rem 43 sts at each shoulder on hold.

FRONT

Return the 126 front sts to the working needle. Work as for back to the 9th row of the 5th repeat of Chart C.

Shape neck

BO the center 14 sts, then, with 2 balls of yarn, work each side separately. On every other row, at neck edge BO 4 sts once, then BO 3 sts once, then BO 2 sts twice, then dec 1 st twice.

When piece measures same as back to shoulders, place rem shoulder sts on hold.

Join front to back at shoulders with three-needle BO or slip-stitch crochet worked tightly.

COLLAR

With RS facing, pick up and knit approx 75 sts around the neck and work 30 rnds of garter st, beginning with a purl rnd.

BO and work 1 rnd of crab stitch (rev single crochet) around the neck edge.

SLEEVES

Put the 13 gusset sts onto a circular needle, and with RS facing, pick up and knit 42 sts along front of armhole and 42 sts along back of armhole and join to work in the round—97 sts. The beg of the rnd is the center st of the gusset. Knit 1 rnd.

Next 2 rnds: Work 39 sts in St st, work the next 20 sts following Chart B2, then work 38 sts in St st.

On the next and every foll 3rd rnd, ssk with the first 2 gusset sts and k2tog with the last 2 gusset sts until only the center "seam stitch" is left. Purl this st every rnd to the cuff.

On the 20th and every foll 5th rnd, dec at beg and end of the round by working k2tog before the seam st and ssk after the seam st until 51 sts rem.

When the sleeve measures 16½ in / 42 cm, and you are on rnd 1 of Chart B2, decrease 4 sts in the cable patt by working k2tog in each of the two-purl columns and at the center of the 2 cable crossings.

Work 20 rnds in garter st, then BO loosely. Work 1 rnd of crab stitch around cuff, as on the neck.

FINISHING

Steam lightly or spray the sweater with water, and dry under a damp towel.

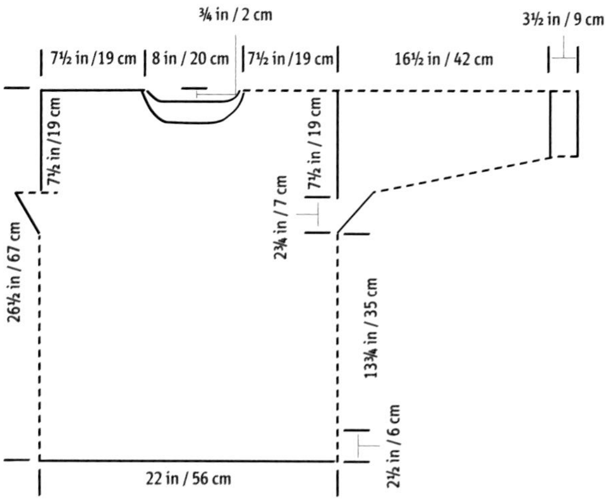

¾ in / 2 cm

3½ in / 9 cm

7½ in /19 cm | 8 in / 20 cm | 7½ in /19 cm

16½ in / 42 cm

7½ in /19 cm

7½ in / 19 cm

2¾ in / 7 cm

26½ in / 67 cm

13¾ in / 35 cm

2½ in / 6 cm

22 in / 56 cm

Western Style

This large shawl adds a touch of Wild West romance to your life and keeps you stylishly warm on every outing.

PATTERN STITCHES

Stockinette Stitch (St st)
Knit RS rows; purl WS rows.

Full-Fashion Increases

Chart A shows only RS rows except for rows 18 and 34. These two WS rows are knitted, and all others are purled. On RS rows, incs are worked as M1, and on WS rows 18 and 34, incs are worked as M1p. No other WS rows have incs. Rows 1-36 are worked once and then Rows 21-36 are repeated while the increases at the left selvage continue throughout.

Full-Fashion Decreases

Chart B shows only RS rows except for rows 170 and 186. These two WS rows are knitted, and all others are purled. On RS rows, decs are worked as k2tog, and on WS rows 170 and 186, decs are worked as p2tog. No other WS rows have decs. Rows 167-202 are worked once and then Rows 187-202. The decreases continue along the left selvage throughout.

INSTRUCTIONS

With Charcoal Gray, CO 3 sts and begin following Chart A working in St st with garter ridges on Rows 18 and 34. Continue to follow the chart, with more sts after each repeat. When piece measures 39¼ in / 100 cm and 166 rows have been worked, the center of the triangle has been reached and a total of 92 incs have been worked—95 sts.

Begin following Chart B, dec as indicated on chart, working in St st with garter ridges on Rows 170 and 186. Cont to foll the chart, with fewer sts rem after each rep.

When 3 sts rem, BO.

LEVEL OF DIFFICULTY

Easy

SIZE

Approx 36¼ x 78¾ in / 92 x 200 cm, excluding fringe

MATERIALS

Yarn: (CYCA #6), Lana Grossa Pernoi (50% virgin wool, 50% acrylic, 99 yd / 50 g), Charcoal Gray Heather 06, 350 g, Camel Heather 10, and Mocha Heather 09, 50 g each
Needles: U.S. size 9 / 5.5 mm: straight and 40 in / 100 cm circular needles or size needed to obtain gauge
Crochet hook: U.S. size N/P-15 / 10 mm

GAUGE

10 sts and 16½ rows in St st = 4 x 4 in / 10 x 10 cm

FINISHING

Wash, pin to measurements, and dry flat to block.

Attach fringe

Cut 2 strands of each color of yarn 13¾ in / 35 cm long for each fringe. Fold the strands in half and attach to the bottom edge of the shawl with the crochet hook.

Chart A

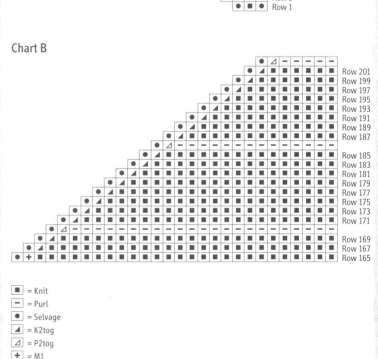

Row 35
Row 33
Row 31
Row 29
Row 27
Row 25
Row 23
Row 21
Row 19
Row 17
Row 15
Row 13
Row 11
Row 9
Row 7
Row 5
Row 3
Row 1

Chart B

Row 201
Row 199
Row 197
Row 195
Row 193
Row 191
Row 189
Row 187
Row 185
Row 183
Row 181
Row 179
Row 177
Row 175
Row 173
Row 171
Row 169
Row 167
Row 165

■ = Knit
− = Purl
● = Selvage
◢ = K2tog
◿ = P2tog
+ = M1
✕ = M1p

24

Instructions on page 26-27

Romantic
capelet with
matching
cuffs

Romantic Capelet with Matching Cuffs

Warm and practical, this duo of capelet and matching cuffs belongs in every wardrobe.

LEVEL OF DIFFICULTY
Intermediate

SIZES
M/L / European 38/40 (42/44)
The numbers for the smaller size are listed first and those for the larger size are within parentheses. When only one number is given, it applies to both sizes.

MATERIALS
Capelet
Yarn: (CYCA #4), Lana Grossa Royal Tweed (100% Pure new Merino wool, 110 yd/101 m / 50g), Olive 96, 200 g
Needles: U.S. size 8 / 5 mm: 32 in / 80 cm circular or size needed to obtain gauge
Cable needle
Separating zipper, 12 in / 30 cm long

Cuffs
Yarn: (CYCA #4), Lana Grossa Royal Tweed (100% Pure new wool, 110 yd / 50 g), Olive 96, 100 g
Needles: U.S. size 8 /5 mm dpn or size needed to obtain gauge
Cable needle

GAUGE
19 sts and 22 rows in Rope Cable = 4 x 4 in / 10 x 10 cm

PATTERN STITCHES
Rope Cables 1 and 2
Wrong side rows are not shown on the charts. On WS rows, knit the knits and purl the purls.
Work the charts for your size. For size M the rep is 12 sts, for size L the rep is 14 sts. Work Rows 1-8 for pattern.

Diamond Cable
Wrong side rows are not shown on the charts. On WS rows, knit the knits and purl the purls. The pattern rep is 24 rows.

K2, P2 Ribbing
Row 1 (RS): (K2, p2) across.
All other rows: Knit the knits and purl the purls.

Garter Ribbing
Rows 1 and 4: Knit.
Rows 2 and 3: Purl.
Rep Rows 1-4 for pattern.

Rope Cable 1: Size M — Row 7, Row 5, Row 3, Row 1 — Cable Patt = 12 sts

Rope Cable 1: Size L — Row 7, Row 5, Row 3, Row 1 — Cable Patt = 14 sts

Rope Cable 2: Size M — Row 7, Row 5, Row 3, Row 1 — Cable Patt = 12 sts

Rope Cable 2: Size L — Row 7, Row 5, Row 3, Row 1 — Cable Patt = 14 sts

Diamond — 23 Row/Rnd, 21 Row/Rnd, 19 Row/Rnd, 17 Row/Rnd, 15 Row/Rnd, 13 Row/Rnd, 11 Row/Rnd, 9 Row/Rnd, 7 Row/Rnd, 5 Row/Rnd, 3 Row/Rnd, 1 Row/Rnd

- = Purl
- = Knit
= Sl 2 sts to cn and hold in back, k2, k2 from cn
= Sl 4 sts to cn and hold in back, k4, k4 from cn
= Sl 2 sts to cn and hold in front, k2, k2 from cn
= Sl 4 sts to cn and hold in front, k4, k4 from cn
= Sl 2 sts to cn and hold in front, p1, k2 from cn
= Sl 1 st to cn and hold in back, k2, p1 from cn

INSTRUCTIONS
SHORT PONCHO
CO 202 (218) sts.

Set up patts as follows:
Knit 1 (selvage), k3, * work 12 (14) sts Rope Cable 1, work 14 sts Diamond, work 12 (14) sts Rope Cable 2, work 14 sts Diamond; rep from * 2 more times, work 12 (14) sts Rope Cable 1, work 14 sts Diamond, work 12 (14) Rope Cable 2, k3, k1 (selvage).

Work even in patts as set until piece measures 11½ in / 29 cm and 64 rows have been worked.

Begin shoulder decs
On Rows 1, 5 and 7 of the Rope Cable charts, dec as foll:
On each rope cable, work the first knit as k2tog (the 1st knit st of the cable and the last purl st before the cable, and on the last st of the cable, work ssk (the last knit st of the cable and the first purl st after the cable)—154 (170) sts rem.
On the next RS row, k2tog 4 times across each 8-st rope cable section—122 sts rem for M.
Next row (size L only): P2tog twice on the 4 rem sts in each rope cable section—124 sts rem.

Collar
Work garter rib pattern and dec as foll in 4th row: (K4, k2tog) 19 times—103 (105) sts rem.

Continue in garter rib until collar measures 3 in / 8 cm. BO loosely.

FINISHING
Wash, pat into shape, and dry flat under a damp towel.
Sew in the zipper, beginning at the neckline.

CUFFS
CO 36 sts. Divide stitches onto 3 dpn (11-14-11) and join to work in the round, being careful not to twist sts. Work Rev St st on needles 1 and 3, and follow the Diamond chart on needle 2.

When knitting measures 6 in / 15 cm, change to k2, p2 ribbing on needles 1 and 3. When ribbing measures 9¾ in / 25 cm, change back to Rev St st on needles 1 and 3.

Thumb opening
Work 2 in (5 cm) in patt, then, when piece measures 11¾ in / 30 cm, on needle 1, BO the center 3 sts. CO 3 over this gap on the next rnd.

When piece measures 13¾ in / 35 cm and 74 rnds have been worked, BO.

Work the second cuff the same way, placing the thumb opening on ndl 3.

FINISHING
Steam lightly or spray the cuffs with water, and dry under a damp towel.

Rustic Pullover

This pullover looks great when paired with a classic skirt and boots or with jeans!

PATTERN STITCHES

K2, P2 Ribbing
Row 1: (K2, p2) across.
All other rows: Knit the knits and purl the purls.

Stockinette Stitch (St st)
Knit the RS rows and purl the WS rows.

Reverse Stockinette Stitch (Rev St st)
Purl the RS rows and knit the WS rows.

Garter stitch
Back and forth: knit all rows.
In the round: *knit 1 rnd, purl 1 rnd and rep from *.

Cable
Wrong side rows are not shown on the charts. On WS rows, knit the knits and purl the purls. Work rows 1 and 2 once, then repeat Rows 3-42 for pattern.

TECHNIQUES

Full-Fashion Decrease 1
Beg of row: Work selvage st, k3, p2tog.
End of row: P2tog, k3, work selvage st.

Full-Fashion Decrease 2
Beg of row: Work selvage st, k1, p2tog.
End of row: P2tog, k1, work selvage st.

Full-Fashion Increase
Beg of row: Work selvage st, k3, M1p.
End of row: M1p, k3, work selvage st.

LEVEL OF DIFFICULTY
Advanced

SIZES
S (M, L) / European 36/38 (40/42, 44/46)
The numbers for the smallest size are listed first and those for the larger sizes are within parentheses. When only one number is given, it applies to all sizes.

MATERIALS
Yarn: (CYCA #5), Lana Grossa Royal Tweed (100% Pure new Merino wool, 110 yd/101 m / 50 g), Camel Heather 64, 450 (500, 550) g
Needles: U.S. sizes 9 and 10 / 5.5 and 6 mm: 24 in / 60 cm circulars; U.S. size 9 / 5.5 mm: 16 in / 40 cm circular or sizes needed to obtain gauge
2 cable needles

GAUGE
14 sts and 20 rows in St st = 4 x 4 in / 10 x 10 cm

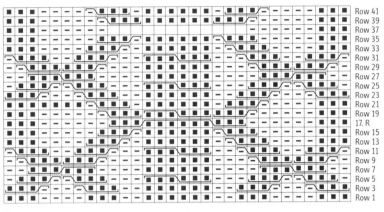

Row 41
Row 39
Row 37
Row 35
Row 33
Row 31
Row 29
Row 27
Row 25
Row 23
Row 21
Row 19
17. R
Row 15
Row 13
Row 11
Row 9
Row 7
Row 5
Row 3
Row 1

■ = Knit

— = Purl

= Sl 3 sts to cn and hold in front, p1, k3 from cn.

= Sl 1 st to cn and hold in back, k3, p1 from cn.

= Sl 3 sts to cn and hold in front, k3, k3 from cn.

= Sl 3 sts to cn and hold in front, sl 6 sts to another cn and hold in back, k3, k6 from 2nd cn and then k3 from 1st cn.

= Sl 3 to cn and hold in front, sl 6 to a second cn and hold in back, k3, k6 from 2nd cn, k3 from first cn.

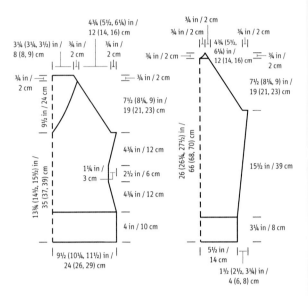

INSTRUCTIONS

BACK

On U.S. size 9 / 5.5 mm long circular, CO 78 (86, 94) sts.

Setup row: K1 (selvage), work 23 (27, 31) sts in k2, p2 ribbing: k1, p2, (k2, p2) 4 (5, 6), work 30 sts over Cable Chart, work 23 (27, 31) sts k2, p2 ribbing: (p2, k2) 4 (5, 6) times, p2, k1, k1 (selvage).

Work 4 in / 10 cm in patts as est, then change to U.S. size 10 / 6 mm ndl.

Setup row: K1 (selvage), work 3 sts in St st, work 20 (24, 28) sts in Rev St st, work 30 sts over Cable Chart, work 20 (24, 28) sts in Rev St st, work 3 sts in St st, k1 (selvage).

Waist shaping

Work in patts as est and dec 1 st inside selvage st at each side every 6th row 4 times, using Full Fashion Decrease 1.

When piece measures 11 in / 28 cm, inc 1 st at each side on the next row and then every foll 6th row 4 times, using Full-Fashion Increase.

Raglan shaping

When piece measures 15¾ in / 40 cm, BO 2 sts at beg of next 2 rows.

Setup row: K1 (selvage), work 1 st in St st, work 20 (24, 28) sts in Rev St st, work 30 sts over Cable Chart, work 20 (24, 28) sts in Rev St st, work 1 st in St st, k1 (selvage).

Work in patt as est and dec 1 st at both ends every other row 21 (23, 25) times using Full-Fashion Decrease 2.

When piece measures 24 (24¾, 25½) in / 61 (63, 65) cm, BO rem 32 (36, 40) sts loosely and, *at the same time*, work k2tog 10 (14, 14) times evenly across the cable panel—22 (22, 26) sts bound off.

FRONT

Work as for back, including all shaping, until piece measures 13¾ (14½, 15½) in / 35 (37, 39) cm. End after working a WS row.

Shape neck

Divide the sts in half at the center.

Left shoulder

Working back and forth on the sts for the left shoulder only, dec 1 st at neck edge every other row 10 (14, 18) times, then every 4th row 6 (4, 2) times.

Raglan shaping

When piece measures 15¾ in / 40 cm in total length, at the armhole edge BO 2 sts once.

From now on, begin RS rows as follows: K1 (selvage), work 1 st in St st, work patts as est across remainder of row.

Dec 1 st at armhole edge every other row 19 (21, 23) times, using Full-Fashion Decrease 2.

When piece measures 23¼ (24, 24¾) in / 59 (61, 63) cm, BO rem 2 sts.

Right shoulder

Reattach yarn at Work as for left shoulder, reversing shaping.

LEFT SLEEVE

With U.S. size 9 / 5.5 mm ndl, CO 42 sts.

Work in garter st for 3¼ in / 8 cm.

Change to U.S. size 10 / 6 mm ndl.
Setup row: K1 (selvage), work 3 sts in St st, work 34 sts in Rev St st, work 3 sts in St st, k1 (selvage).

When piece measures 8 in / 20 cm, inc 1 st inside edge st at each side of next row, and then on every 16th (10th, 8th) row 2 (5, 6) times, then in every 6th row 2 (2, 4) times using Full-Fashion Increase—52 (58, 64) sts.

Raglan shaping

When piece measures 18½ in / 47 cm, BO 2 sts each at beg of next 2 rows.
Setup row: K1 (selvage), work 1 st in St st,

work 44 (50, 56) sts in Rev St st, work 1 st in St st, k1 (selvage).

Continue working patts as est and dec 1 st at both ends every other row 19 (21, 23) times using Full-Fashion Decrease 2. Then on the left edge only, on the next row BO 2 (4, 6) sts, then every other row BO 3 sts twice.

RIGHT SLEEVE

Work as for Left Sleeve, reversing shaping.

FINISHING

Sew the side seams, sleeve seams, and raglan seams.

With RS facing and the short U.S. size 9 / 5.5 mm ndl, pick up and knit approx 103 sts around neck opening. Work garter stitch in the round and, *at the same time*, k3tog at the center front every other rnd.

When neck band measures 1½ in / 4 cm, dec 8 times evenly around. Repeat decs once more on next knit rnd if desired for a closer fit. When neck band measures 2 in /5 cm, BO all sts.

Relaxing Knitwear

Knitting is the new yoga. Even when you're working on a project, you're relaxed. And when the garment is finished, it envelops you and invites you to simply switch off and let your mind wander. Try it and create your own personal wellness outfit!

Delicate Lace

Big needles and chunky yarn make this sweater a quick knit while the feminine lace pattern and fashionable ribbing create a sophisticated and elegant look.

LEVEL OF DIFFICULTY
Intermediate

SIZES
S (M) / European 36/38 (40/42)
The numbers for the smaller size are listed first and those for the larger size are within parentheses.

When only one number is given, it applies to both sizes.

MATERIALS
Yarn: (CYCA #4), Lana Grossa Superbingo (100% Merino wool; 88 yd/80 m / 50 g), Dark Gray 25, 650 (700) g
Needles: U.S. sizes 10 and 10½ / 6

and 6.5 mm: 24 in / 60 cm circulars; U.S. size 10 / 6 mm: 16 in / 40 cm circular or sizes needed to obtain gauge

GAUGE
13 sts and 20 rows in Lace Pattern = 4 x 4 in / 10 x 10 cm using larger needles

PATTERN STITCHES
K1, P1 Rib (worked over an odd number of sts)
Row 1 (RS): (K1, p1) to last st, k1.
All other rows: Knit the knits and purl the purls.

Lace Pattern
Wrong side rows are not shown on the chart. Purl all WS rows. Rep Rows 1-16 for pattern.

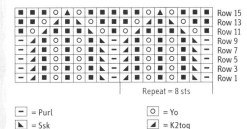

Repeat = 8 sts

☐ = Purl
◣ = Ssk
■ = Knit
○ = Yo
◢ = K2tog

INSTRUCTIONS

BACK
With longer size 10 / 6 mm needle, CO 59 (67 sts)
Work in K1, p1 ribbing for 4¾ in / 12 cm. End after working a WS row. Change to larger needle.
Setup row: K1 (selvage), work Lace Chart rep patt 7 (8) times across to last st, k1 (selvage).
For size S only: Beg with chart Row 1 and rep Rows 1-16 for pattern.
For size M only: Beg with Row 11; work Rows 11-16 once, then rep Rows 11-16 for patt.

Neck shaping
When piece measures 22½ (23½) in / 57 (60) cm, BO the center 21 sts and beg working both shoulders separately with 2 balls of yarn. Continue working patt as est, and *at the same time*, on the next RS row dec 1st at

neck edge twice.
When piece measures 23¼ (24½) in / 59 (62) cm, loosely BO the rem 17 (21) sts.

FRONT
Work as for back until piece measures 20½ (21½) in / 52 (55) cm.

Neck shaping
BO the center 17 sts and begin working both shoulders separately with 2 balls of yarn. Continue working patt as est, and, *at the same time*, at beg of next two RS rows, BO 2 sts each.
When piece measures 23¼ (24½) in / 59 (62) cm, loosely BO the rem 17 (21) sts.

SLEEVES
With smaller needle, CO 33 sts.
Work in ribbing for 4¾ in / 12 cm. On

the last row (WS), inc 1 st each side—35 sts.

Change to larger ndl.

Setup row: K1 (selvage), work Lace Chart rep pattern 4 times across to last st, k1 (selvage). Continue working in patt as est, increasing 1 st inside selvage st at each side every 16th (12th) row 4 (6) times, working all incs into Lace patt—43 (47) sts

Shape sleeve cap

When piece measures 20½ in / 52 cm, BO 2 sts at beg of next 2 rows and then, on every other row, BO 2 sts 3 times. When sleeve measures 22 in / 56 cm BO rem 27 (31) sts.

FINISHING

Sew shoulder seams.

With the short circular needle and RS facing, pick up and knit approx 68 sts around neck opening.

Join, purl 1 rnd, and then work in k1, p1 ribbing for 1¼ in /3 cm).

BO loosely in pattern.

Sew side seams up to under-arm, leaving 7 (7½) in / 18 (19) cm open for armhole. Sew sleeve seams. Set sleeves into armholes.

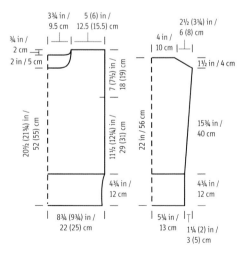

Warm and
Elegant
Instructions on pages 38-39

Warm and Elegant

This cardigan is a great beginner project, the stretchy pattern uses only knit and purl stitches!

PATTERN STITCHES

Chart shows RS and WS rows. Rep Rows 1 and 2 for pattern.

Work back and forth following the chart. Work the sts as shown. Begin RS rows at right side of chart and beg WS rows at left side of chart. Beg the row with the sts before the repeat, work the repeat, and end the row with the sts after the repeat. Repeat Rows 1-2 for pattern.

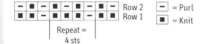

TECHNIQUES

Full-Fashion Decreases

At the beginning of the row, after the selvage st, decrease using ssk.
At the end of the row, decrease using k2tog before the selvage st.
Purl the resulting stitch on the following WS row.

INSTRUCTIONS

BACK

CO 41 (45, 49) sts and begin working in charted pattern.
When piece measures 15¼ (15¾, 16¼) in / 39 (40, 41) cm and 50 (52, 54) rows have been worked, place markers at each side for armholes.
Work even until the armholes measures 6¼ (6¾, 7) in / 16 (17, 18 cm) or 22 (24, 26) rows.

Neck shaping

BO the center 15 sts and beg working each shoulder separately.
Work even for ¾ in / 2 cm, then loosely BO the rem 13 (15, 17) sts.

LEFT FRONT

CO 21 (23, 25) sts and beg working in charted pattern, ending with 3 (1, 3) sts after the rep.

Neck shaping

When piece measures 12¾ (13½, 14¼) in / 32 (34, 36) cm and 42 (46, 50) rows have been worked, beg working neck shaping on the left edge of the piece.

On the next row, and every foll 4th row, decrease 1 st 7 times using the Full Fashion Decrease. *At the same time*, pm for armhole when the piece measures same as back to marker.

LEVEL OF DIFFICULTY

Easy

SIZES

S (M, L) / European 36/38 (40/42, 44/46)
The numbers for the smallest size are listed first and those for the two larger sizes are within parentheses. When only one number is given, it applies to all sizes.

MATERIALS

Yarn: (CYCA #6), Lana Grossa Lei (100% Merino wool; 43 yd/39 m / 50 g), Charcoal 32, 550 (660, 650) g
Needles: U.S. size 17 / 12.75 mm: 32 in / 80 cm circular or size needed to obtain gauge
Crochet hook: U.S. size K-10½ / 6.5 mm
Notions: 1 button in a matching color, approx 1½ in / 3.8 cm in diameter

GAUGE

8.5 sts and 13 rows in Charted Pattern = 4 x 4 in / 10 x 10 cm

When shoulder measures same as back, loosely BO rem sts.

RIGHT FRONT
Work as for Left Front, reversing shaping.

SLEEVES
CO 21 (25, 25) sts and beg working in charted pattern.
Inc at each side on the 5th row and then on every 10th (12th, 10th) row 5 (4, 5) times, working all incs into charted patt—33 (35, 37) sts.
Note: Work incs as M1 after the first st of the row and before the last st of the row.

When piece measures 19 in / 48 cm or 62 rows, BO loosely.

FINISHING
Wet pieces, pin to dimensions, and dry flat to block. Sew the side seams up to the armhole markers. Sew the sleeve seams.
On the right front, work 1 row of single crochet, making a 6-chain loop at the base of the neck shaping for a buttonhole loop.
Set in sleeves. Sew on button.

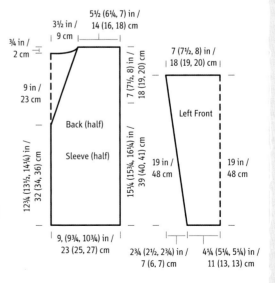

5½ (6¼, 7) in /
14 (16, 18) cm

3½ in /
9 cm

¾ in /
2 cm

9 in /
23 cm

7 (7½, 8) in /
18 (19, 20) cm

Back (half)

Sleeve (half)

12¾ (13½, 14¼) in /
32 (34, 36) cm

15¼ (15¾, 16¼) in /
39 (40, 41) cm

9, (9¾, 10¾) in /
23 (25, 27) cm

7 (7½, 8) in /
18 (19, 20) cm

Left Front

19 in /
48 cm

19 in /
48 cm

2¾ (2½, 2¾) in /
7 (6, 7) cm

4¼ (5¼, 5¼) in /
11 (13, 13) cm

Feminine Favorite

A classic tweed yarn knit in a cable and lace pattern make this traditional vest a stylish and timeless must-have.

LEVEL OF DIFFICULTY
Advanced

SIZES
S / European 38

MATERIALS
Yarn: (CYCA #4), Lana Grossa

Windsor (55% Merino wool, 31% mohair, 14% polyamide; 120 yd/110 m / 50 g)
MC Blue Heather 01, 400 g
CC Navy Blue Heather 04, 50 g
Needles: U.S. size 6 / 4 mm: two 24 in / 60 cm circulars or size needed to obtain gauge

Crochet hook: U.S. size G-6 / 4 mm
Cable needle

GAUGE
19 sts and 29 rows in St st and braid cables patt = 4 x 4 in / 10 x 10 cm when lightly stretched

PATTERN STITCHES

Stockinette Stitch (St st)
Back and forth: Knit RS rows; purl WS rows.
In the round: Knit all rnds.

Background Pattern
Work in St st interspersed with 6-st columns of Braid Pattern as noted in instructions.

Cable Border Pattern
Every row is shown on the chart.
Work Rnds 1-16 once.

Braid Pattern
Even rows are not shown on the chart. On even rnds, knit the knits and yarnovers, and purl the purls as stitches face you.

■ = Knit

– = Purl

○ = Yo

◣ = Ssk

◢ = K2tog

▩▩▩▩▩ = Sl 2 sts to cn and hold in front, k2, k2 from cn

☐ = No stitch

↓ ↓ ↓ ↓ = Sl 4 sts to cn, wrap the working yarn around these sts 3 times to form a cluster, sl the 4 sts onto the right ndl

Chart A

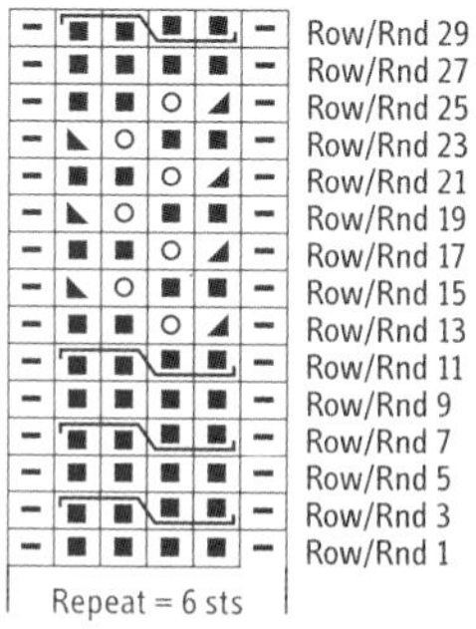

Row/Rnd 29
Row/Rnd 27
Row/Rnd 25
Row/Rnd 23
Row/Rnd 21
Row/Rnd 19
Row/Rnd 17
Row/Rnd 15
Row/Rnd 13
Row/Rnd 11
Row/Rnd 9
Row/Rnd 7
Row/Rnd 5
Row/Rnd 3
Row/Rnd 1

Repeat = 6 sts

Chart B

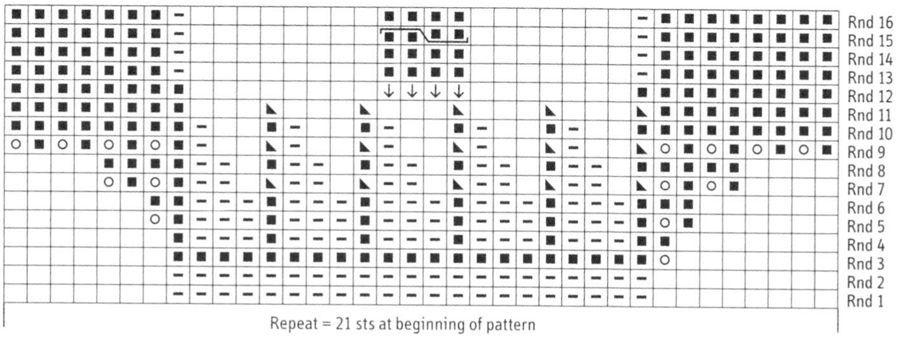

Rnd 16
Rnd 15
Rnd 14
Rnd 13
Rnd 12
Rnd 11
Rnd 10
Rnd 9
Rnd 8
Rnd 7
Rnd 6
Rnd 5
Rnd 4
Rnd 3
Rnd 2
Rnd 1

Repeat = 21 sts at beginning of pattern

INSTRUCTIONS

This vest is worked to the armholes in one piece in the round.

CO 168 sts.
Purl 1 row (RS) then join to work in the rnd, being careful not to twist sts.

Work all rows of Border (Chart B), beg with Row 2 of chart.

Beg working in St st, *but*, over the center 6 sts of each border repeat, work the Braid Pattern (Chart A).
On the 6th rnd, then every 12th rnd 6 times, move the 1st and 5th braids 1 st to the left as foll: Work up to 2 sts before the braid, M1, work the 6 sts of Chart A, k1, ssk and, *at the same time*, move the 4th and 8th braids 1 st to the right as foll: Work up to 3 sts before the braid, k2tog, k1, work the 6 sts of Chart A, k1, M1.

When piece measures 11¾ in / 30 cm and 79 rnds have been worked after edging, divide at armholes for front and back as follows:
Front: Work across the first 85 sts (braid strips 1-4 and 15 sts at each side edge).
Back: Place the next 83 sts (braid strips 5-8 and 14 sts at each side edge) on a spare ndl or st holder.

Note: On both front and back, knit the first st of every row for a selvage.

FRONT

Work back and forth on the 85 front sts.

Armhole shaping

BO 3 sts each at beg of next 2 rows twice and then BO 2 sts each at beg of next 2 rows once, then BO 1 st at beg of next 2 rows twice—5 sts rem before braid 1 and after braid 4.

Work even until piece measures 14¼ in / 36.5 cm. End after working a WS row.

Neck shaping

On the next row, BO the center 15 sts and work each shoulder separately. Every other row, at the neck edge BO 6 sts once, then BO 3 sts once.
When piece measures 20½ in / (52 cm, place rem 16 sts on hold.

BACK

Return the 83 Back sts to the working needle.

Armhole shaping

BO 3 sts at beg of next 2 rows, then BO 2 sts at beg of next 2 rows twice, then BO 1 st at beg of next 2 rows twice—5 sts rem before braid 5 and after braid 8.

Work even until piece measures 19½ in / 50 cm. End after working a WS row.

Neck shaping

On the next row, BO the center 21 sts and work each shoulder separately. Every other row, at the neck edge BO 6 sts once.
When piece measures 20½ in / 52 cm, place rem 16 sts on hold.

FINISHING

Join shoulders with three-needle bind- off or Kitchener st. Steam or spray vest and allow it to dry under a damp towel.
With CC, work 1 rnd of single crochet and 1 rnd of crab stitch around the armholes and neckline. If the edge rolls, press it lightly under a damp pressing cloth.

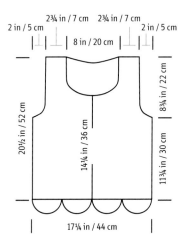

2 in / 5 cm   2¾ in / 7 cm   2¾ in / 7 cm   2 in / 5 cm
8 in / 20 cm
8¾ in / 22 cm
20½ in / 52 cm
14¼ in / 36 cm
11¾ in / 30 cm
17¼ in / 44 cm

Figure-Flattering Vest

Instructions on pages 44-45

Figure-Flattering Vest

This lovely vest compliments everyone's figure, its shape and drape will flatter your feminine curves.

LEVEL OF DIFFICULTY
Easy

SIZES
S (M, L) / European 36/38 (40/42, 44/46)
The numbers for the smallest size are listed first and those for the two larger sizes are within parentheses. When only one number is given, it applies to all sizes.

MATERIALS
Yarn: (CYCA #6), Lana Grossa Lei (100% Merino wool; 43 yd/39 m / 50 g), Khaki 27, 600 (650, 700) g

Needles: U.S. sizes 13 and 15 / 9 and 10 mm: 24 in / 60 cm circulars or sizes needed to obtain gauge
Crochet hook: U.S. Size M/N-13 / 9 mm

GAUGE
9 sts and 14 rows in St st = 4 x 4 in / 10 x 10 cm using larger needles

PATTERN STITCHES
K1, P1 Ribbing
Row 1 (RS): (P1, k1) to last st, p1.
All other rows: Knit the knits and purl the purls.

Stockinette Stitch (St st)
Knit RS rows and purl WS rows.

TECHNIQUES
Chain selvage
Ever row: Knit the 1st st through the back loop, slip the last stitch pwise wyif.

INSTRUCTIONS
Front and back are worked tog as one piece. Arrows on the schematic show the direction of knitting.

LEFT FRONT
Beg at the left front edge, with larger circular, CO 50 (52, 54) sts.

Set up row: Slip 1 (selvage), work 41 (43, 45) sts in St st, work 7 sts in K1, P1 ribbing, beg and ending with a purl, k1 (selvage).

The ribbing creates the front bands and neck band.

When piece measures 19½ (20, 20½) in / 50 (51, 52) cm and 70 (72, 74) rows have been worked, shape armhole.

Armhole shaping
Work 19 (20, 21) sts, then BO 18 (19, 20) sts as foll:
Slip the first 2 sts to the right ndl, then pass the second st over the first. *Slip the next st on the left ndl to the right ndl , then pass the second st on the right ndl over the first. Repeat from * until all 18 (19, 20) sts have been bound off. Place the last st on the right ndl back onto the left ndl.

Cast on 18 (19, 20) sts to replace the bound-off sts as foll: use the crochet hook to chain 18 (19, 20), working into the last live st on the next ndl to begin the chain. Put the last chain onto the right ndl and work in patt as est to the end of the row.

BACK
Next row (WS): Work in patt as est

and then pick up and knit 1 st each in the back of 17 (18, 19) crochet chains.

Work in patt as est until Back measures 12 (12½, 13½) in / 30 (32, 34) cm and 42 (44, 48) rows have been worked.

Work second armhole as the first.

Right Front

Work even in patts as est until piece measures same as Left Front. BO all sts loosely kwise on RS.

FINISHING

Wash and dry flat to block.

With smaller needles, and RS facing, pick up and knit 39 (43, 47) sts over the center 15¾ (17¼, 18¾) in / 40 (44, 48) cm of the lower back edge.

Setup row: Slip 1 (selvage), (p1, k1) to last 2 sts, p1, k1 (selvage).

Work in ribbing with chain selvage until piece measures 8¼ in / 21 cm from pick up row and 29 rows of ribbing have been worked. BO all sts in patt.

For the ties, work two crochet chains approx 15¾ in / 40 cm long. With crochet hook, work 1 row of crab stitch around armholes.

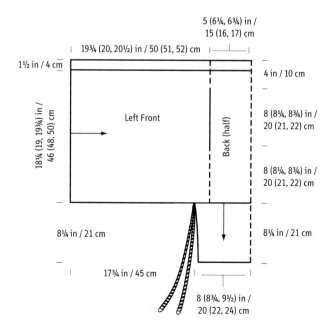

5 (6¼, 6¾) in / 15 (16, 17) cm

19¾ (20, 20½) in / 50 (51, 52) cm

1½ in / 4 cm

4 in / 10 cm

18¼ (19, 19¾) in / 46 (48, 50) cm

Left Front

Back (half)

8 (8¼, 8¾) in / 20 (21, 22) cm

8 (8¼, 8¾) in / 20 (21, 22) cm

8¼ in / 21 cm

8¼ in / 21 cm

17¾ in / 45 cm

8 (8¾, 9½) in / 20 (22, 24) cm

Vintage-style Shoulder Wrap

Super soft yarn and thicker needles combine to create a wonderfully airy and fine knitted fabric that keeps you warm.

PATTERN STITCHES

Garter stitch
Knit every row.

Crochet Edging
1 Chain
1 Single crochet
1 Double crochet
Garter ridge

Selvage
Knit the first and last stitch of every row.

INSTRUCTIONS

This shawl is knit from side to side. The arrow on the schematic shows the direction of knitting.

CO 5 sts and work back and forth in garter stitch.
Inc at the end of every RS row 80 times as foll: Knit to last st, yo, k1 (selvage)—85 sts.

Work even for 7 in / 18 cm.
At the center of the shawl, the piece measures 29½ in / 75 cm from the cast-on row.

Work even for 7 in / 18 cm.

Now shape the other side of the shawl by dec at the end of every RS row 80 times as follows: Knit to last 3 sts, k2tog, k1 (selvage)—5 sts. BO.

FINISHING

Work the crochet edging as charted, skipping 4 rows (2 garter ridges) between each stitch, to prevent the edge from curling.

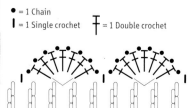

● = 1 Chain
I = 1 Single crochet   ⊤ = 1 Double crochet

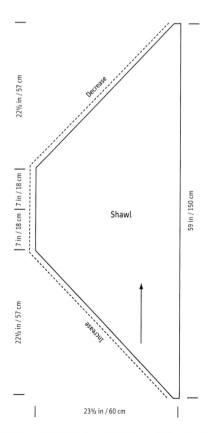

22½ in / 57 cm

Decrease

7 in / 18 cm | 7 in / 18 cm

Shawl

59 in / 150 cm

22½ in / 57 cm

Increase

23½ in / 60 cm

LEVEL OF DIFFICULTY
Easy

SIZE
50 x 24 in / 150 x 60 cm

MATERIALS
Yarn: (CYCA #4), Lana Grossa Silkhair (70% mohair, 30% silk; 229 yd/209 m / 25 g), Taupe 29, 75 g
Needles: U.S. size 7 / 4.5 mm: 32 in / 80 cm circular or size needed to obtain gauge
Crochet hook: U.S. size 7 / 4.5 mm

GAUGE
14 sts and 28 rows in garter stitch = 4 x 4 in / 10 x 10 cm

Outdoor Jacket with Cables

If it's still a bit too chilly outside for a light cardigan, but also rather warm for a fall jacket, then this cabled sweater jacket should be just right for long walks.

LEVEL OF DIFFICULTY
Advanced

SIZES
S (M, L) / European 36/38 (40/42, 44/46)
The numbers for the smallest size are listed first and those for the two larger sizes are within parentheses.

When only one number is given, it applies to all sizes.

MATERIALS
Yarn: (CYCA #5), Lana Grossa Bingo Print (100% Merino wool; 88 yd/ 80 m / 50 g), Light/Medium/Dark Brown 607, 850 (900, 950) g
Needles: U.S. sizes 7 and 9 / 4.5 and

5.5 mm: 24 in / 60 cm circulars or sizes needed to obtain gauge
Cable needle
6 buttons in a matching color, approx 1 in / 2.5 cm in diameter

GAUGE
16 sts and 23 rows in Rev St st = 4 x 4 in / 10 x 10 cm using larger needles

PATTERN STITCHES
K1, P1 Ribbing
Row 1 (RS): (K1, p1) across.
All other rows: Knit the knits and purl the purls.

Stockinette Stitch (St st)
Knit RS rows; purl WS rows.

Reverse Stockinette Stitch (Rev St st)
Purl RS rows; knit WS rows.

Cable Pattern
Wrong side rows are not shown on the charts. On WS rows, knit the knits and purl the purls as sts face you.

INSTRUCTIONS

BACK
With larger ndl, CO 106 (112, 118) sts.
Setup row: K1 (selvage), work 10 (13, 16) sts Rev St st, * work 15 sts over Cable Chart, work 8 sts Rev St st, rep from * 2 more times, work 15 sts Cable Chart, work 10 (13, 16) sts Rev St st, k1 (selvage).
Work first cable crossing after row 10.

Waist shaping
When piece measures 2¾ (3¼, 3½) in / 7 (8, 9) cm, dec 1 st at each side on the next row, then every following 6th row 5 times.

Work 7 rows even.
Inc at each side on the next row then every 6th row 4 times—104 (110, 116) sts.

Armhole shaping
When piece measures 14½ (15, 15¾) in / 37 (38, 39) cm, BO 3 sts at beg of next 2 rows, then BO 2 sts at beg of next 2 rows, then dec 1 st at each side on every other row 2 (3, 4) times—90 (94, 98) sts rem.

When armhole measures 7¾ (8¼, 8¾) in / 20 (21, 22) cm, BO rem sts loosely, and, *at the same time*, in the center of each cable, k3tog.

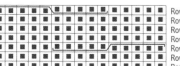
Cable Patt = 15 sts

Row 15
Row 13
Row 11
Row 9
Row 7
Row 5
Row 3
Row 1

■ = Knit
= Sl 5 sts to cn and hold in back, k5, k5 from cn
= Sl 5 sts to cn and hold in front, k5, k5 from cn

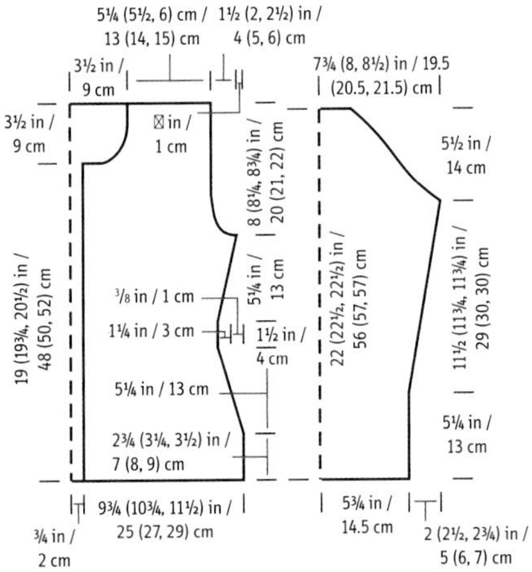

Work waist and armhole shaping on the right edge of the piece as for back.

Neck shaping

When piece measures 19 (19½, 21) in / 48 (50, 52) cm, on the left edge of the piece, BO 7 sts for the neck edge once, then every other row, BO 3 sts once then 2 sts twice, then on the 4th row dec 1 st once.

When armhole measures 8 (8¼, 8¾) in / 20 (21, 22) cm BO rem 28 (30, 32) sts loosely, and, *at the same time*, in the center of each cable, k3tog.

RIGHT FRONT

Work as for Left Front, reversing shaping.

SLEEVES

With larger needle, CO 53 sts.
Setup row: K1 (selvage), work 18 sts Rev St st, 15 sts Cable Patt, 18 sts Rev St st, k1 (selvage).

When piece measures 5 in / 13 cm, on next row, inc 1 st inside edge st at each side.
Next, working all incs as Rev St st, inc 1 st at each side:
For S only: Every 8th row 7 times
For M only: Alternating between every 6th and every 8th row 9 times
For L only: Every 6th row 10 times
For all sizes, when all incs have been completed—69 (73, 75) sts.

Sleeve cap shaping

When sleeve measures 16½ (17, 17) in (42, 43, 43) cm, BO 3 (3, 4) sts each at beg of next 2 rows, then BO 2 sts each at

beg of next 2 rows twice, then dec 1 st at beg and end of every other row 11 (10, 10) times. Next, BO 1 (2, 2) sts at beg of next 2 rows twice and then BO 4 sts at beg of next 2 rows once.
BO rem 21 (23, 23) sts loosely and, *at the same time*, k3tog at center of cable.

FINISHING

Wash pieces and lay flat to block.
Sew shoulder seams.

Neckband

With smaller needle and RS facing, pick up and knit approx 75 sts around neck opening and work in k1, p1 ribbing for 3½ in / 9 cm. BO all sts loosely in patt.

Buttonhole Band

With smaller needle and RS facing, pick up and knit approx 103 (107, 111) sts and work in k1, p1 ribbing.

When band measures ¾ in / 2 cm, BO 2 sts for buttonhole 2½ in / 6 cm from the neck edge and again for 5 more buttonholes spaced approx 3 (3¼, 3¼) in / 7.5 (8, 8) cm apart. On the next row, CO 2 sts over each buttonhole and resume working in patt.
When band measures 1½ in / 4 cm from buttonholes, BO all sts in patt.

Button Band

Work left front band as for right front band but without buttonholes.
Sew on buttons.

Sew side and sleeve seams and set sleeves into armholes.

Schematic measurements

5¼ (5½, 6) cm / 13 (14, 15) cm   1½ (2, 2½) in / 4 (5, 6) cm

3½ in / 9 cm

☒ in / 1 cm

7¾ (8, 8½) in / 19.5 (20.5, 21.5) cm

3½ in / 9 cm

8 (8¼, 8¾) in / 20 (21, 22) cm

5½ in / 14 cm

19 (19¾, 20½) in / 48 (50, 52) cm

⅜ in / 1 cm

1¼ in / 3 cm

5¼ in / 13 cm

1½ in / 4 cm

5¼ in / 13 cm

2¾ (3¼, 3½) in / 7 (8, 9) cm

22 (22½, 22½) in / 56 (57, 57) cm

11½ (11¾, 11¾) in / 29 (30, 30) cm

5¼ in / 13 cm

¾ in / 2 cm

9¾ (10¾, 11½) in / 25 (27, 29) cm

5¾ in / 14.5 cm

2 (2½, 2¾) in / 5 (6, 7) cm

LEFT FRONT

With larger needle, CO 54 (57, 60) sts.
Setup row: K1 (selvage), work 10 (13, 16) sts Rev St st, work 15 sts over Cable Chart, Work 8 sts Rev St st, work 15 sts over Cable Chart, work 4 sts Rev St st, k1 (selvage).
Work first cable crossing after row 10.

Finely Wrapped

Instructions on pages 52-53

Finely Wrapped
Wrap garments offer comfort and layering, as well as fitting a variety of figures.

PATTERN STITCHES

Garter stitch
Knit all rows.

Stockinette Stitch (St st)
Knit RS rows; purl WS rows.

TECHNIQUES

Full-Fashion Decreases
At the beginning of the row, after the selvage st, decrease using ssk.
At the end of the row, decrease using k2tog before the selvage st. Purl the resulting stitch on the following WS row.

INSTRUCTIONS

Sleeves are worked in one piece with Back and Fronts.

BACK

CO 86 (94, 102) sts.
Work in garter stitch for 5 rows or ³⁄₈ in / 1 cm, beg with a WS row. Change to St st and continue working back and forth to sleeves.

Sleeves

When piece measures 8 (8¼, 8¾) in / 20 (21, 22) cm and 66 (70, 74) rows have been worked, inc 1 st inside selvage at each side on the next and then every other row once. Next CO 2 sts at beg of next 2 rows 4 times, then CO 5 sts at beg of next 2 rows once—116 (124, 132) sts.

Work even until sleeve measures 6¼ (6¾, 7) in / 16 (17, 18) cm and 52 (56, 60) rows have been worked after last cast-on row.

Shape shoulders

BO 6 (7, 7) sts at beg of next 2 rows, then BO 6 sts at beg of next 2 rows 4 times. Next, BO 5 (6, 7) sts at beg of next 2 rows 3 (7, 4) times, then BO 6 sts beg of next 2 rows 3 times.

LEVEL OF DIFFICULTY

Easy

SIZES

S (M, L) / European 36 (40, 44)
The numbers for the smallest size are listed first and those for the two larger sizes are within parentheses. When only one number is given, it applies to all sizes.

MATERIALS

Yarn: (CYCA #3), Lana Grossa Solo Cashmere 110 (100% Cashmere; 120 yd/110 m / 25 g), Taupe 117, 175 (200, 225) g
Needles: U.S. size 4 / 3.5 mm: 32 in / 80 cm circular or size needed to obtain gauge

GAUGE

21 sts and 33 rows in St st = 4 x 4 in / 10 x 10 cm

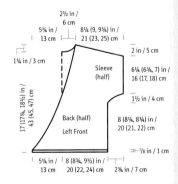

At the same time, when making the 4th shoulder dec, BO the center 6 sts for the neck and begin working each side separately. At the neck edge, every other row BO 4 sts once, then BO 3 sts twice.

When all sts on first shoulder have been bound off, work second shoulder the same way, reversing shaping.

LEFT FRONT
CO 72 (76, 80) sts.
Work in garter stitch for 5 rows or 3/8 in / 1 cm, beg with a WS row.
Change to St st.
For the front edge shaping, using full-fashion decreases and beg on the 3rd row, dec 1 st inside selvage at left edge once, then dec every other row 24 times; every 4th row 10 times, then every 6th row 7 times. Work sleeve and shoulder shaping on the right edge to match the back, using up all sts.

RIGHT FRONT
Work as for Left Front, reversing shaping.

FINISHING
Wash pieces and dry flat to block.
Sew the shoulder seams.

Left Band
With RS facing and starting in the center of the back neck opening, pick up and knit 112 (116, 120) sts along the left side of the back neck and down the left front, then CO 105 sts—217 (221, 225 sts total).
Beg with a WS row, work in St st for 2¼ in / 5.5 cm. BO.

Right Band
CO 105 sts, then with RS facing and starting at the bottom right-front edge, pick up and knit 112 (116, 120) sts along the right front edge and across the right half of the back neck.

Sew center back seam on bands.

Armhole Edging
With RS facing, pick up and knit 68 (72, 76) sts around armhole opening. Work 5 rows in garter st. BO.

Sew the sleeve and underarm seams.

Showpieces

A stylish woman simply can't have too many knitted accessories. Hats, scarves, mittens and more are available in countless shapes, colors and yarns. Since small projects are quick to knit, you can easily select projects to match your personal style.

Autumn Inspiration

Made in the vibrant colors of autumn, these pieces are not worked in the traditional flat or circular fashion, but in modular knit triangles.

LEVEL OF DIFFICULTY
Easy

SIZES
Hat circumference: 21¼—22¾ in / 54—58 cm
Scarf: 6¾—7 in / 17—18 cm and 55 in / 140 cm long

MATERIALS
Yarn: (CYCA #6), Lana Grossa Elle (58% acrylic, 42% virgin wool; 43 yd/39 m / 50 g), Orange 04, 150 g for the hat; 350 g for the scarf
Needles: U.S. size 13 / 9 mm: 24 in / 60 cm circular or size needed to obtain gauge

GAUGE
9 sts and 18 rows in Garter Stitch = 4 x 4 in / 10 x 10 cm

To make a straight scarf, do not sew the ends together. You can make as many triangles as you want.

PATTERN STITCHES
Garter stitch
Back and forth: knit all rows.

TECHNIQUES
Selvage
Knit the first and last stitch of every row for selvage.

INSTRUCTIONS

COWL
The arrows on the schematic show the direction of knitting.

CO 26 sts and work back and forth in garter stitch as foll:

*Row 1: Knit.
Row 2: Knit to last 2 sts, k2tog.
Rep last 2 rows until 1 st rem.

For the next triangle, pick up and knit 25 sts along the diagonal edge of the previous triangle (26 sts total).

Rep from * until you have 8 triangles.
Sew the ends of the piece together to form a circle.

HAT
The arrow on the schematic shows the direction of knitting. CO 33 sts and work in garter stitch as foll:

Row 1: Knit.
Row 2: K1, yo, knit to the last 2 sts, k2tog.
Row 3: Knit to last 2 sts, knit the yo through back loop, k1.
The stitch count should remain constant at 33 sts.
Rep Rows 2 and 3 until piece measures 19¾ in / 50 cm.
BO but do not fasten off. Run the yarn through the sts on the upper edge of the piece and gather together to shape hat. Fold and arrange brim as desired.

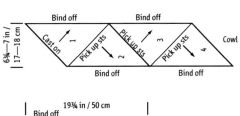

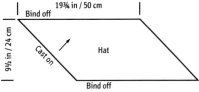

It's Teatime!

English country chic knit in trendy berry colors!

LEVEL OF DIFFICULTY
Intermediate

SIZES
Hat circumference: 21¼—22 in /
54—56 cm

MATERIALS
Yarn: (CYCA #3), Lana Grossa Windsor
(55% Merino wool, 31% mohair, 14%
polyamide; 120 yd/110 m / 50 g);
Blackberry 03, 100 g
Needles: U.S. size 8 / 5 mm: set of 5 dpn
or size needed to obtain correct gauge
Cable needle

Notions: Grosgrain ribbon, 24 in / 60 cm
long or length to fit around your head +
¾ in / 2 cm

GAUGE
24 sts and 24 rnds in Cable Pattern =
4 x 4 in / 10 x 10 cm

PATTERN STITCHES
Stockinette Stitch (St st)
Knit all rnds.

Cable
Wrong side rows are not shown on the
chart. On WS rows, knit the knits and
purl the purls as sts face you. Repeat
Rows 1-8 for pattern.

Crown Shaping
All rnds are shown on the chart.
Work Rnds 1-16 once to shape
the crown.

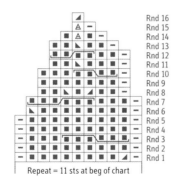

Repeat = 11 sts at beg of chart

■ = Knit

— = Purl

△ = Sl 2-k1-p2sso

◣ = Sl 1-k1-psso

◢ = K2tog

▨ = Sl 2 sts to cn and hold in back, k2,
k2 from cn

▨ = Sl 2 sts to cn and hold in front, k2,
k2 from cn

▨ = Sl 3 sts to cn and hold in
back, k3, k3 from cn

▨ = Sl 3 sts to cn and hold in
front, k3, k3 from cn

INSTRUCTIONS
CO 100 sts. Distribute sts evenly on 4 dpn and
join to work in the round, being careful not to
twist, Knit 2 rnds.
Rnd 3: (K5, M1) 20 times—120 sts.
When brim measures 2 in / 5 cm, purl 1 rnd
for turning ridge.
Work even in St st for 2 in / 5 cm.
Begin Cable pattern, working 12-st rep 10
times around.
After Rnd 32 (piece measures approx 5 in /
13 cm), begin following Crown Shaping chart.

When 10 sts rem, cut the yarn and run the tail
through the rem sts. Pull gently to fasten off
and weave in ends neatly on WS.

FINISHING
Put the grosgrain ribbon around your head to
determine a comfortable length. Cut it about
¾ in / 2 cm longer, overlap the ends, and sew
the ribbon into a circle.
Turn up the brim at the turning ridge. Place
the ribbon inside the brim and sew the hem
in place.

Cheeky Cables

Warm ear flaps with ties and a sideways-knit cable border make this hat cozy and warm.

LEVEL OF DIFFICULTY
Easy

SIZE
Hat circumference: 21¼—22 in / 54—56 cm

MATERIALS
Yarn: (CYCA #3), Lana Grossa Windsor (55% Merino wool, 31% mohair, 14% polyamide; 120 yd/110 m / 50 g); Beige Heather 07, 100 g
Needles: U.S. size 8 / 5 mm: set of 5 dpn or size needed to obtain gauge
Cable needle

GAUGE
24 sts and 24 rnds in Cable pattern = 4 x 4 in / 10 x 10 cm

PATTERN STITCHES
K2, P2 Ribbing
All rnds: (K2, p2) around.

Cable
Wrong side rows are not shown on the chart. On WS rows, knit the knits and purl the purls as sts face you. Repeat Rows 1-8 for pattern.

INSTRUCTIONS
The cable border is worked back and forth in rows and the ends are sewn together to form a ring. Stitches are picked up on the side of the border along the selvedge and the hat is knit up to the crown.

Row 7
Row 5
Row 3
Row 1

Repeat = 12 sts

□ = Purl

■ = Knit

= Sl 3 sts to cn and hold in back, k3, k3 from cn

= Sl 3 sts to cn and hold in front, k3, k3 from cn

CABLE BORDER
CO 25 sts.
Row 1 (RS): K1 (selvage), work 12- st repeat of Cable chart twice.
Work in patt as est until piece measures 21 in / 53 cm and 128 rows have been worked.
BO. Sew short ends of band together to form a ring.

HAT
With RS facing, pick up and knit 128 sts along the selvage of the cable border.
Work in k2, p2 ribbing until piece measures 3¼ in / 8 cm.
Next rnd: (K2, p2tog) around—96 sts rem.
Next 3 rnds: (K2, p1) around.
Next rnd: (K1, k2tog) around—64 sts rem.
Change to St st and place marker after every 8th st.
Next rnd: Knit.
Next rnd: (Knit until 2 sts before marker, k2tog).
Rep last 2 rnds until 8 sts rem.
Cut the yarn and draw the tail through the rem sts. Pull gently to fasten off and weave in ends neatly on WS.

Ear flaps
On the bottom edge of the Cable Border, with RS facing, beg 16 rows from the seam and pick up and knit 24 sts.
Setup row (WS): K1 (selvage), (p2, k2) to last 3 sts, p2, k1 (selvage).
Work even in Ribbing with selvage until flap measures 1¼ in / 3 cm.
Dec row (RS): K1 (selvage), p2, k2tog, work in ribbing to last 5 sts, k2tog, p2, k1 (selvage)—22 sts rem.
Rep dec row every 4th row twice—18 sts rem.
Rep dec row every other row 7 times—4 sts rem.
Work 4-st I-cord as follows:
*Knit 4, do not turn. Slide 4 sts to other end of dpn and draw yarn tightly across the back. Rep from * until cord measures 6 in / 15 cm.
BO. Tug gently on the cord to even out the stitches.

Make a second ear flap on the opposite side of the hat.

Fine Neck Warmer

The elegant **colors**, the simple but effective brioche pattern, and the original shaping combine to make this scarf an absolute favorite.

LEVEL OF DIFFICULTY
Intermediate

SIZE
9¾ in / 25 cm wide and 24 in / 60 cm long after joining into loop

MATERIALS
Yarn: (CYCA #4), Lana Grossa Alpina (80% virgin wool, 20% polyamide; 263 yd/240 m / 100 g), Ecru 10 and Light Gray 04, 100 g each
Needles: U.S. size 7 / 4.5 mm: 24 in / 60 cm circular or size needed to obtain gauge
Notions: Shawl pin

GAUGE
16 sts and 32 rows in Brioche stitch = 4 x 4 in / 10 x 10 cm

PATTERN STITCHES

Brioche Selvage
The first and last 3 sts of each row are not worked in patt, but as follows: Knit the knits and slip the purls wyif.

Brioche (worked with an even number of stitches)
Row 1 (RS): K1 (selvage), * p1, k1, rep from * across and end k1 (selvage).
Row 2 (WS): Work 3-st Brioche selvage, * sl 1, yo, k1; rep from * to last 3 sts, work 3-st Brioche selvage.
Row 3 (and all following rows): Work 3-st Brioche selvage, * sl, yo, k2tog (yo and slipped stitch from previous row); rep from * to last 3 sts, work 3-st Brioche selvage.

INSTRUCTIONS

With Ecru, CO 22 sts and work in Brioche patt for 2 in / 5 cm. Put sts on hold.
Rep from * to * once more.
Put all 44 sts tog on one needle and work across all sts in Brioche stitch, decreasing on the first row as foll: work the last 2 sts of the first piece tog in pattern, then work the first 2 sts of the second piece tog in pattern—42 sts rem.
Cont to work Brioche patt across all sts until piece measures 12 in / 30 cm, then change to Light Gray.
Work in patt as est until piece measures a total of 24 in / 60 cm.
Next row: Work 3-st Brioche selvage, (p3tog, work 1 Brioche st) across to last 3 sts, work 3-st brioche selvage—24 sts rem.
Work even for 6 in / 15 cm. BO loosely.

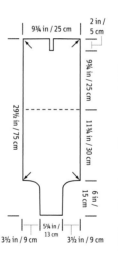

FINISHING
Sew the CO ends together as shown on the schematic. Sew the sides of the scarf below the narrow end together for a few in (cm) to prevent curling. Pull the scarf end through the opening and secure the scarf with the shawl pin.

Cozy Tam

The Tam combines a trendy look with cozy tweed yarn, a striking accessory for any season.

LEVEL OF DIFFICULTY
Intermediate

SIZE
Hat circumference: 21¼–22 in / 54–56 cm

MATERIALS
Yarn: (CYCA #4) Lana Grossa Windsor (55% Merino wool, 31% mohair, 14% polyamide; 120 yd 110 m / 50 g); in Green/Olive Heather 05, 150 g
Needles: U.S. size 8 / 5 mm: 16 in /40 cm circular or size needed to obtain gauge
Cable needle

GAUGE
24 sts and 24 rnd in Cable pattern = 4 x 4 in / 10 x 10 cm

PATTERN STITCHES

K2, P2 Ribbing
All rounds: (K2, p2) around.

Cable
Wrong side rows are not shown on the chart. On WS rows, knit the knits and purl the purls as sts face you.

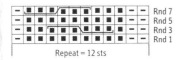

Repeat = 12 sts

■ = Knit
– = Purl
▲ = Sl 2-k1-p2sso
◣ = Ssk
◢ = K2tog

Crown Shaping

All rnds are shown on the chart. Work Rnds 1-16 once to shape the crown.

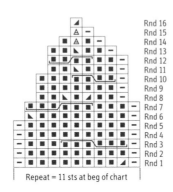

Rnd 16
Rnd 15
Rnd 14
Rnd 13
Rnd 12
Rnd 11
Rnd 10
Rnd 9
Rnd 8
Rnd 7
Rnd 6
Rnd 5
Rnd 4
Rnd 3
Rnd 2
Rnd 1

Repeat = 11 sts at beg of chart

= Sl 2 sts to cn and hold in back, k2, k2 from cn

= Sl 2 sts to cn and hold in front, k2, k2 from cn

= Sl 3 sts to cn and hold in back, k3, k3 from cn

= Sl 3 sts to cn and hold in front, k3, k3 from cn

INSTRUCTIONS

CO 96 sts and join to work in the round, being careful not to twist sts. Work in k2, p2 ribbing for 2 in / 5 cm.

Inc rnd: K1, (M1, k2) 47 times, M1—144 sts

Work 12 reps of 12-st Cable chart around.

When Cable section measures 2¾ in / 7 cm, inc in each 3-purl column as follows: p1, M1p, p1, M1p, p1—168 sts and 5 purls between each cable.

When Cable section measures 6 in / 15 cm, dec as follows: work the last purl in each column together with the first cable stitch as k2tog and work the last cable stitch with the following purl as ssk—144 sts.

When Cable section measures 8 in / 20 cm and 48 rows have been worked, change to Crown Shaping chart. After last rnd of chart is worked, 12 sts rem. Cut yarn, draw the tail through the rem sts and pull gently to fasten off. Weave in ends neatly on WS.

FINISHING

Dampen the hat, stretch it over a plate or a cardboard circle approx 9½ in / 24 cm in diameter and allow it to dry thoroughly.

On Foot

Hand-knitted socks are classic knitting projects. Whether you're wearing hiking boots in a rustic woodland, working in the garden in rubber boots, or snuggling in front of the fireplace, nothing warms our feet as well as socks knitted with cozy yarn. These patterns are so beautiful, it's a shame to hide them in shoes!

Cozy Spa Socks

You'll want to have these socks ready after a long day at work. The super soft yarn will make your feet feel better in no time at all.

LEVEL OF DIFFICULTY
Intermediate

SIZE
Women's medium/men's small
(European 38/39)

MATERIALS
Yarn: (CYCA #3), Lana Grossa
Merino Superfine (100% Merino
wool; 175 yd/160 m / 50 g), Olive
101, 150 g
Needles: U.S. size 2-3 / 3 mm: set of
5 dpn or size needed to obtain
gauge

Cable needle

GAUGE
24 sts and 33 rows in St st = 4 x 4 in
/ 10 x 10 cm

PATTERN STITCHES
Cuff pattern
All rnds: (K2, p2) around for
ribbing.

Diamond Cable for Instep
Work all rnds as charted,
repeating Rows 1-16 of chart
for pattern.

Back Leg Pattern
Work all rnds as charted,
repeating Rows 1-14 of chart
for pattern.

Stockinette Stitch (St st)
Back and forth: Knit RS rows;
purl WS rows.
In the round: knit all rounds.

Diamond Cable for Instep

Rnd 16
Rnd 15
Rnd 14
Rnd 13
Rnd 12
Rnd 11
Rnd 10
Rnd 9
Rnd 8
Rnd 7
Rnd 6
Rnd 5
Rnd 4
Rnd 3
Rnd 2
Rnd 1

Back Leg Pattern

Rnd 14
Rnd 13
Rnd 12
Rnd 11
Rnd 10
Rnd 9
Rnd 8
Rnd 7
Rnd 6
Rnd 5
Rnd 4
Rnd 3
Rnd 2
Rnd 1

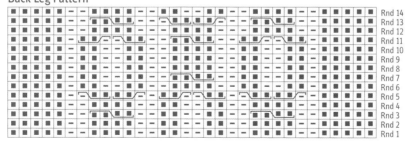

─ = Purl

■ = Knit

= Sl 2 sts to cn and hold in
front, k2, k2 from cn

= Sl 2 sts to cn and hold in front, p1, k2
from cn

= Sl 1 st to cn and hold in back, k2, p1
from cn

= Sl 1 st to cn and hold in front, k1, k1 from cn

= Sl 1 st to cn and hold in back, k1, k1 from cn

= Sl 1 st to cn and hold in back, k1, p1 from cn

= Sl 1 st to cn and hold in front, p1, k1 from cn

INSTRUCTIONS

CO 64 sts.
Divide sts onto 4 dpn (16 sts on each ndl) to work in the rnd, being careful not to twist sts.

CUFF

Work in k2, p2 ribbing for 4 in / 10 cm.
Knit 1 rnd.

LEG

Beg working Diamond Cable chart over sts on ndls 1 and 2 and Back Leg chart over sts on ndls 3 and 4.
Work in patts as est until all 16 rnds of Diamond Cable chart have been worked twice.

HEEL

Rnd 33: Work in patt and, *at the same time,*

over the first 12 sts on needle 3 *and* over the last 12 stitches on ndl 4, k2tog twice—these 28 sts now form the heel.
Set aside the sts on needles on ndls 1 and 2.

Heel Flap

Maintain the cable pattern down the center 8 sts of the heel and work the remainder of the sts in St st with garter selvages for 26 rows.

Heel Turn

Row 1 (RS): K16, ssk, k1, turn.
Row 2 (WS): Sl 1 pwise, p5, p2tog, p1, turn.
Row 3: Sl 1 kwise, knit to 1 st before gap, ssk (working 1 st before and 1 st after gap tog), k1, turn.
Row 4: Sl 1 pwise, purl to 1 st before gap, p2tog, p1, turn.
Rep rows 3 and 4 until 16 sts rem.
K8. Place marker for beginning of rnd.

INSTEP

Return to working in the rnd and rearrange sts on Rnd 1 as foll:
Ndl 1: K8, pick up and knit 12 sts along side of heel flap, M1 between needles 1 and 2.
Ndls 2 and 3: Work Diamond Cable patt as est.
Ndl 4: M1 between needles 3 and 4, pick up and knit 12 sts along side of heel flap, k8.

Rnd 2: K21 sole sts, work Diamond Cable patt as est on ndls 2 and 3, k21 sole sts.
Rnd 3: Work in patt as est and, *at the same time,* dec as foll: with the last st of ndl 1 and the 1st twisted st of the Diamond Cable, sl 1

pwise, sl 1 kwise, put the 2 slipped stitches back onto the left needle, then k2tog (twisted right-slanting dec); with the last twisted st of the Diamond Cable and the first st on ndl 4 tog as k2tog tbl (twisted left-slanting dec)—2 sts decreased.
Rnd 4: Work in St st over the sole sts and Diamond Cable patt over the instep sts.
Repeat Rnds 3 and 4 until 60 sts rem (32 sts on top of foot in Diamond Cable patt and 28 sts on sole in St st).

FOOT

Work even in patt as est until 5 repeats of the Diamond Cable have been completed below the ribbed cuff.
On the next rnd dec 4 sts on the instep—56 sts. Divide sts evenly onto 4 dpn (14 sts per ndl).

TOE

Work the Band Toe as follows:
Dec 1: *On ndl 1, k to last 3 sts, k2tog, k1; on ndl 2, k1, ssk, knit to end of ndl; rep from * on ndls 3 and 4.
Dec as above on the 4th rnd once, on the 3rd rnd once, every other rnd 3 times, then every rnd 4 times.
On the next rnd, work k2tog with the last 2 sts on ndls 1 and 3 and ssk with the first 2 sts on ndls 2 and 4.
Divide the sts into 2 equal sections with 8 sts each and join with Kitchener st.

Make the second sock the same way.

Casual
Checks

Instructions on page 72

Casual Checks

Planning a relaxing weekend on the couch with lots of hot chocolate and a good book? If so, this is the right pair of socks for you to slip on and be cozy!

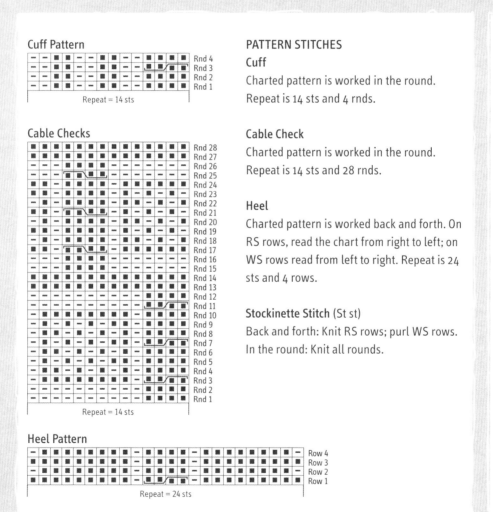

Cuff Pattern

Repeat = 14 sts
Rnd 1 / Rnd 2 / Rnd 3 / Rnd 4

Cable Checks

Repeat = 14 sts
Rnd 1 – Rnd 28

Heel Pattern

Repeat = 24 sts
Row 1 / Row 2 / Row 3 / Row 4

■ = Knit on RS, purl on WS

– = Purl on RS, knit on WS

■■■■ = Sl 2 sts to cn and hold in back, k2, k2 from cn

■■■■ = Sl 2 sts to cn and hold in front, k2, k2 from cn

PATTERN STITCHES

Cuff
Charted pattern is worked in the round.
Repeat is 14 sts and 4 rnds.

Cable Check
Charted pattern is worked in the round.
Repeat is 14 sts and 28 rnds.

Heel
Charted pattern is worked back and forth. On RS rows, read the chart from right to left; on WS rows read from left to right. Repeat is 24 sts and 4 rows.

Stockinette Stitch (St st)
Back and forth: Knit RS rows; purl WS rows.
In the round: Knit all rounds.

LEVEL OF DIFFICULTY
Intermediate

SIZE
Women's medium/ men's small / European 38/40

MATERIALS
Yarn: (CYCA #3), Lana Grossa Cool Wool Melange (100% Merino wool; 175 yd/160 m/50 g), Bark 115, 100 g
Needles: U.S. size 2-3 / 3 mm: set of 5 dpn or size needed to obtain gauge
Cable needle

GAUGE
22 sts and 32 rows in St st = 4 x 4 in / 10 x 10 cm

INSTRUCTIONS

CO 56 sts and divide sts evenly over 4 dpn (14 sts per ndl). Join to work in the rnd, being careful not to twist sts.

CUFF

Work charted Cuff pattern for 16 rnds.

LEG

Work Rows 1-28 of Cable Checks patt once, then work Rows 1-14 again—42 rnds total.

In the next rnd, work in patt as est over ndls 1 and 2 and the first 4 sts of ndl 3. Set these 32 sts aside.

HEEL

The heel is worked back and forth on the rem 24 sts on ndls 3 and 4.

Heel Flap

Work Rows 1-4 of Heel Chart (working garter st selvages) 6 times—24 rows total.

Heel Turn

Row 1 (RS): K14, ssk, k1, turn.
Row 2 (WS): Sl 1 pwise, p5, p2tog, p1, turn.
Row 3: Sl 1 kwise, knit to 1 st before gap, ssk (working 1 st before and 1 st after gap tog), k1, turn.
Row 4: Sl 1 pwise, purl to 1 st before gap, p2tog, p1, turn.
Rep Rows 3 and 4 until 14 sts rem.
K7. Place marker for beginning of rnd.

INSTEP

Return to working in the rnd and rearrange sts on Rnd 1 as foll:

Ndl 1: K7, pick up and knit 12 sts in the garter bumps along side of heel flap.
Ndls 2 and 3: Work patt as est.
Ndl 4: Pick up and knit 12 sts along side of heel flap, k7.

Rnds 2 and 3: Knit sole sts on ndl 1; work patt as est on ndls 2 and 3; knit sole sts on ndl 4.
Rnd 4: K to last 3 sts on ndl 1, k2tog, k1; work patt as est on ndls 2 and 3; on ndl 4 k1, ssk, knit to end of rnd.

Rep rnds 3 and 4 six times—56 sts rem (24 sole sts worked in St st, 32 instep sts worked in patt).

FOOT

Work even in patt as est until 54 rnds have been completed (ending with the 12th rnd of the 4th repeat).

TOE

Divide sts evenly onto 4 ndls and work the Band Toe as follows:
Dec 1: *On ndl 1, k to last 3 sts, k2tog, k1; on ndl 2, k1, ssk, knit to end of ndl; rep from * on ndls 3 and 4.
Dec as above on the 4th rnd once, on the 3rd rnd twice, every other rnd 3 times, then every rnd until 5 sts rem on each ndl.
On the next rnd, work k2tog with the last 2 sts on ndls 1 and 3 and ssk with the first 2 sts on ndls 2 and 4.
Divide the sts into 2 equal sections of 8 sts each and join with Kitchener st.

Make the second sock the same way.

A Touch of England

These tweedy socks will remind you of the English countryside, fragrant roses, and a roaring fireplace.

PATTERN STITCHES

Faux Cable Ribbing for Cuff

All rows are shown on the chart. The repeat is 4 sts and 4 rnds.

■ = Knit

─ = Purl

= Sl 1 pwise wyib, k1, yo, k1, psso

Ribbing

All rnds: (P1, k3) around.

Cable Pattern

Work following the chart, repeating Rnds 1-11.

─ = Purl

◆ = K1tbl

= Sl 1 st to cn and hold in front, p1, k1tbl from cn

= Sl 1 st to cn and hold in back, k1tbl, p1 from cn

= Sl 1 st to cn and hold in back, k1tbl, k1tbl from cn

= Sl 1 st to cn and hold in front, k1tbl, k1tbl from cn

Stockinette Stitch (St st)

Back and forth: Knit RS rows; purl WS rows.
In the round: knit all rounds.

LEVEL OF DIFFICULTY

Advanced

SIZE

Women's medium/men's small /
European 38/40

MATERIALS

Yarn: (CYCA #2), Lana Grossa Meilenweit 6-ply tweed (80% virgin wool, 20% polyamide; 143 yd/131 m / 50 g /), Natural 8817, 150 g
Needles: U.S. size 2-3 / 3 mm: set of 5 dpn or size needed to obtain gauge
Cable needle

GAUGE

26 sts and 33 rows in St st = 4 x 4 in /
10 x 10 cm

The cable is arranged differently on the right and left socks. The instructions for both socks are the same except as noted in the pattern.

INSTRUCTIONS

CO 60 sts and divide sts over 4 dpn (16-20-12-12). Join to work in the rnd, being careful not to twist sts.

CUFF

Work in 28 rnds in Faux Cable Ribbing.

LEG

On the next 4 rnds, work Faux Cable Ribbing over 1st through 9th rib columns, and work the rest of the sts in p1, k3 ribbing.

On the next 4 rnds, work Faux Cable Ribbing over 2nd through 8th rib columns, and work the rest of the sts in p1, k3 ribbing.

On the next 4 rnds, work Faux Cable Ribbing over 3rd through 7th rib columns, and work the rest of the sts in p1, k3 ribbing.

On the next 4 rnds, work Faux Cable Ribbing over 4th through 6th rib columns, and work the rest of the sts in p1, k3 ribbing.

On the next 4 rnds, work Faux Cable Ribbing over the 5th rib columns, and work the rest of the sts in p1, k3 ribbing.

On the next 4 rnds, work all sts in p1, k3 ribbing.

HEEL

Work the first 4 sts of next rnd 1 onto ndl 4, then work 29 sts in ribbing as est, and put the last 3 sts of ndl 2 onto ndl 3.

The heel is worked back and forth over the 31 sts on ndls 3 and 4. Set rem sts aside.

Heel Flap

Work 26 rows in Ribbing as est.

Heel Turn

Row 1 (RS): K18, ssk, k1, turn.
Row 2 (WS): Sl 1 pwise, p6, p2tog, p1, turn.
Row 3: Sl 1 kwise, knit to 1 st before gap, ssk (working 1 st before and 1 st after gap tog), k1, turn.

Row 4: Sl 1 pwise, purl to 1 st before gap, p2tog, p1, turn.
Rep rows 3 and 4 until 19 sts rem.
K10. Place marker for beginning of rnd.

INSTEP

Return to working in the rnd and rearrange sts on Rnd 1 as foll:
Ndl 1: K9, pick up and knit 13 sts in the garter bumps along side of heel flap, M1 between ndls 1 and 2—23 sts on ndl 1.
Ndls 2 and 3: Work Ribbing as est.
Ndl 4: M1 between needles 2 and 3, then pick up and knit 12 sts along side of heel flap, k10—23 sts on ndl 4 (75 sts total).

LEFT SOCK

Rnd 2: Work 21 sole sts in St st, dec with last 2 sts on ndl 1 (sl 1 kwise, sl1 pwise, put 2 slipped sts back onto left needle, k2tog), work 29 sts in Ribbing as est, dec as above, work next 12 sts in Cable patt, k1tbl, k8.
Rnd 3: Work all sts in patts as est.
Rnd 4: Work 20 sts in St st, dec with last 2 sts on ndl 1 as in Rnd 2, work 28 sts in Ribbing as est, dec, work 12 sts in Cable patt, k1tbl, k8.
Rnd 5: Work as for Rnd 3.
Rnd 6: Work 19 sts in St st, dec with last 2 sts on ndl 1 as in Rnd 2, work 27 sts in Ribbing as est, dec, work 12 sts in Cable patt, k1tbl, k8.
Rep Rnds 5 and 6 with fewer sts in Ribbing and St st sections until 58 sts rem.

Cable Offset Rounds

Move the cable panel diagonally across the foot by working patts as est and, *at the same time*, alternate between working as follows every rnd and every other rnd: With the last st before the cable panel and the first twisted st of the cable panel sl 1 pwise, sl 1 kwise, put sts back on left needle and k2tog (twisted left-leaning dec); after the last st of the cable panel, M1.

RIGHT SOCK

Rnd 2: K8, k1tbl, work 12 sts in Cable patt, k2tog tbl, work 29 sts in Ribbing as est, k2tog tbl, k21.

Rnd 3: Work all sts in patt as est.

Rnd 4: K8, k1tbl, work 12 sts in Cable patt, k2tog tbl, work 28 sts in Ribbing as est, k2tog tbl, k20.

Rnd 5: Rep rnd 3.

Rnd 6: K8, k1tbl, work 12 sts in Cable patt, k2tog tbl, work 27 sts in Ribbing as est, k2tog tbl, k19.

Rep rnds 5 and 6 with fewer sts in Ribbing and St st sections until 58 sts rem.

Cable Offset Rounds

Move the cable panel diagonally across the foot by working patts as est and, *at the same time*, alternate between working as follows every rnd and every other rnd: Before the first twisted st in the cable panel, M1; with the last twisted st of the cable panel and the first st after the cable panel, k2tog tbl.

BOTH SOCKS

Repeat the dec and inc sections until the cable panel has crossed over all of the sts on the top of the foot except for the last knit st.

The last offset rnd is the third rnd of the cable patt repeat.

TOE

Next rnd: Knit, dec evenly spaced around to 56 sts.

Divide sts on 4 dpns (14 sts on each needle) and continue in St st.

Work the Band Toe as follows:

Dec 1: *On ndl 1, k to last 3 sts, k2tog, k1; on ndl 2, k1, ssk, knit to end of ndl; rep from * on ndls 3 and 4.

Dec as above on the 3rd rnd twice, every other rnd 3 times, then every rnd 4 times.

On the next rnd, work k2tog with the last 2 sts on ndls 1 and 3 and ssk with the first 2 sts on ndls 2 and 4.

Divide the sts into 2 equal sections with 8 sts each and join with Kitchener st.

Framed in Pearls

The simple cable panel on these socks is cleverly framed and proceeds all the way to the tip of the toe.

LEVEL OF DIFFICULTY
Advanced

SIZE
Women's medium/men's small / European 38-40

MATERIALS
Yarn: (CYCA #3) Lana Grossa Cool-Wool 2000 (100% Merino wool, 175 yd/160 m / 50 g) Gold-brown 513, 150 g
Needles: U.S size 2-3 / 3 mm: set of 5 dpn or size needed to obtain gauge
Cable needle

GAUGE
24 sts and 33 rows in St st = 4 x 4 in / 10 x 10 cm

PATTERN STITCHES
Channel Island Cast-On
Pull out a tail of yarn approx twice as long as you need for casting on. Double the yarn by folding it in half.

Make a slip knot with both strands of yarn, approx 6 in (12 cm) from the end of the double tail. Hold the tail in your left hand and the single yarn attached to the ball in your right hand.

*YO with the single yarn. While holding the yo in place with your right hand, take the double tail in your left hand and wrap it counter-clockwise around your thumb, twice.
Insert the right needle underneath both strands around your thumb (the single strand yo is still in front of the needle). Take the single strand, and wrap it around the needle as if you were knitting the stitch and pull tightly—2 sts made. Rep from * alternating between yo and k sts, to the desired number of sts CO.

Garter stitch
In the round: *Knit 1 rnd, purl 1 rnd and rep from *.

Top of Foot (Instep)
Work all rnds as charted. Repeat Rnds 1-12 for pattern.

Back of Leg
Work all rnds as charted. Repeat Rnds 1-12 for pattern.

Toe
Work all rnds as charted. Work Rnds 57-75 once.

Seed Stitch
Setup rnd: (K1, p1) around.
All other rnds: Purl the knits and knit the purls.

Cable Heart Pattern for Front of Leg and Instep

Rnd 12
Rnd 11
Rnd 10
Rnd 9
Rnd 8
Rnd 7
Rnd 6
Rnd 5
Rnd 4
Rnd 3
Rnd 2
Rnd 1

Pattern repeat = 32 sts

Back Leg Pattern

Rnd 12
Rnd 11
Rnd 10
Rnd 9
Rnd 8
Rnd 7
Rnd 6
Rnd 5
Rnd 4
Rnd 3
Rnd 2
Rnd 1

Pattern repeat = 32 sts

Toe Pattern

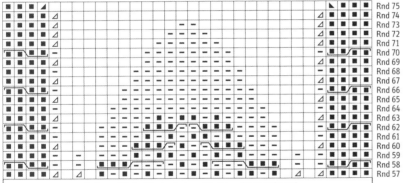

Rnd 75
Rnd 74
Rnd 73
Rnd 72
Rnd 71
Rnd 70
Rnd 69
Rnd 68
Rnd 67
Rnd 66
Rnd 65
Rnd 64
Rnd 63
Rnd 62
Rnd 61
Rnd 60
Rnd 59
Rnd 58
Rnd 57

Pattern = 32 sts at the beginning of the toe and 8 sts at the end

■ = Knit

− = Purl

◢ = K2tog

◿ = P2tog

◣ = Ssk

= Sl 2 sts to cn and hold in front, k2, k2 from cn

= Sl 2 sts to cn and hold in back, k2, k2 from cn

= Sl 1 st to cn and hold in back, k3, p1 from cn

= Sl 3 sts to cn and hold in front, p1, k3 from cn

= Sl 3 sts to cn and hold in front, k3, k3 from cn

= Sl 3 sts to cn and hold in back, k3, k3 from cn

= Sl 3 sts to cn and hold in back, k2, then from cn p1, k2

= Sl 3 sts to cn and hold in front, p3, k3 from cn

= Sl 3 sts to cn and hold in back, k3, p3 from cn

⊡ = Sl 1 pwise wyib

INSTRUCTIONS

CO 60 sts using the Channel Island cast-on. Divide sts evenly over 4 dpn (15 sts per ndl). Join to work in the rnd, being careful not to twist sts.

CUFF

Work 5 rnds garter stitch in the round (alternating knit and purl rnds).
In the next rnd, inc 5 sts evenly spaced around—65 sts.

LEG

Setup rnd: Work Back Leg Chart over 33 sts on ndls 1 and 2, and work Front Cable Heart Chart over 32 sts on ndls 3 and 4.
Work rnds 1-12 of both patts 3 times, then Rnds 1-11 once more.
Rnd 12: On the Back Leg patt, knit the center 5 sts. Work 4 more rnds in patt, working the center 5 sts of back leg patt as St st.

At the first cable crossing after the middle 5 sts are worked in St st, dec as foll: sl 2 sts to cable needle and hold in back, k2tog, k1, k2 from cable needle. Continue working these sts as St st with a cable crossing every 4th rnd.

Set aside the sts on ndls 3 and 4.

HEEL

The heel is worked back and forth on the sts on ndls 1 and 2.

Heel Flap

Work in St st with garter selvages and, *at the same time,* on the first row of the heel, with the 9th and 10th sts and the 23rd and 24th sts, k2tog—30 sts rem in heel.

Work back and forth until 28 rows have been completed.

Heel Turn
Row 1 (RS): K17, ssk, k1, turn.
Row 2 (WS): Sl 1 pwise, p5, p2tog, p1, turn.
Row 3: Sl 1 kwise, knit to 1 st before gap, ssk (working 1 st before and 1 st after gap tog), k1, turn.
Row 4: Sl 1 pwise, purl to 1 st before gap, p2tog, p1, turn.
Rep Rows 3 and 4 until 18 sts rem.
K9. Place marker for beginning of rnd.

INSTEP
Return to working in the rnd and rearrange sts on Rnd 1 as foll:
Ndl 1: K9, pick up and knit 14 sts in the garter bumps along side of heel flap.
Ndls 2 and 3: Work Patt as est.
Ndl 4: Pick up and knit 14 sts along side of heel flap, k9.

Rnds 2 and 3: Knit sole sts on ndl 1; work patt as est on ndls 2 and 3; knit sole sts on ndl 4.

Rnd 4: K to last 3 sts on ndl 1, k2tog, k1; work patt as est on ndls 2 and 3; on ndl 4 k1, ssk, knit to end of rnd.

Rep rnds 3 and 4 eight times—60 sts rem.

FOOT
Work even in est patterns until 56 rnds have been completed.

TOE
Work sole sts in St st and top of toe following Toe Chart. Work the Band Toe with decreases as charted *and* as follows:
On the first toe rnd, work to the last knit st of the sole on ndl1 and knit that stitch tog with the first cable stitch, work in patts as charted to the last cable st on ndl 3 and knit that st tog with the following knit st through the back.

After all rows of chart are worked, 16 sts rem. Divide into 2 sections of 8 sts and join with Kitchener st.

Make the second sock the same way.

Sensual Rosewood

Seductive and romantic, these soft, cuddly socks are knit in a delicate shade of rosewood.

PATTERN STITCHES

Cuff Pattern
K1 twisted, p1 Ribbing
All rnds: (K1tbl, p1) around.

Cable and Slip Stitch Pattern
Work all rnds as charted. The repeat is 20 sts. Repeat Rnds 1-32 for pattern.

Heel Stitch
The heel is worked back and forth. Read Row 1 of chart (RS) from right to left and Row 2 of chart (WS) from left to right. Work the 2-st repeat to the last st, then work the final st of the chart. Repeat Rows 1 and 2 for pattern.

Stockinette Stitch (St st)
Back and forth: Knit RS rows; purl WS rows. In the round: knit all rounds.

LEVEL OF DIFFICULTY
Advanced

SIZE
Women's medium/ men's small / European 38-40

MATERIALS
Yarn: (CYCA #3), Lana Grossa Merino Superfine (100% Merino wool; 175 yd/160 m / 50 g), Rosewood 565, 150 g
Needles: U.S size 2-3 / 3 mm: set of 5 dpn or size needed to obtain gauge
Cable needle

GAUGE
24 sts and 33 rows in St st = 4 x 4 in / 10 x 10 cm

Cable and Slip Stitch

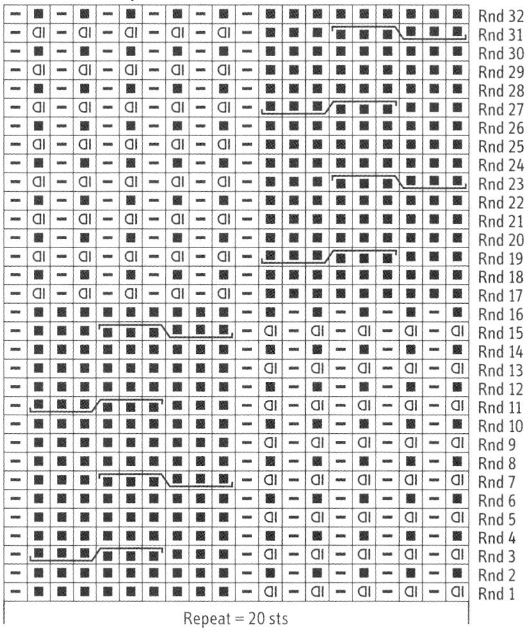

Rnd 32
Rnd 31
Rnd 30
Rnd 29
Rnd 28
Rnd 27
Rnd 26
Rnd 25
Rnd 24
Rnd 23
Rnd 22
Rnd 21
Rnd 20
Rnd 19
Rnd 18
Rnd 17
Rnd 16
Rnd 15
Rnd 14
Rnd 13
Rnd 12
Rnd 11
Rnd 10
Rnd 9
Rnd 8
Rnd 7
Rnd 6
Rnd 5
Rnd 4
Rnd 3
Rnd 2
Rnd 1

Repeat = 20 sts

Heel Stitch

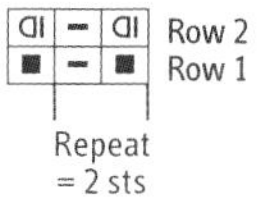

Row 2
Row 1

Repeat = 2 sts

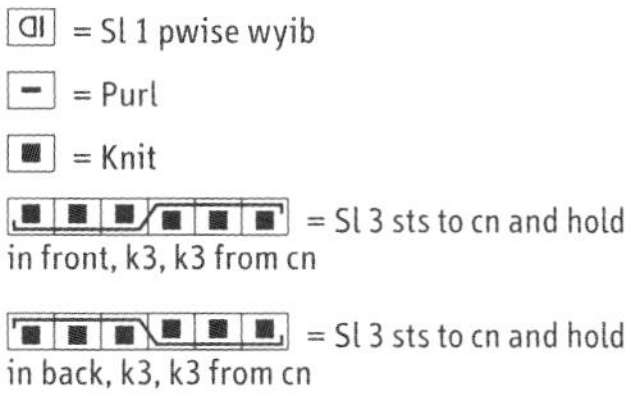

☐ = Sl 1 pwise wyib

− = Purl

■ = Knit

= Sl 3 sts to cn and hold in front, k3, k3 from cn

= Sl 3 sts to cn and hold in back, k3, k3 from cn

INSTRUCTIONS

CO 60 sts and divide sts evenly over 3 dpn (20 sts per ndl). Join to work in the rnd, being careful not to twist sts.

CUFF

Work in k1tbl, p1 ribbing for 12 rnds.

LEG

Work rows 1-32 rows of Cable pattern once, then work Rows 1-16 again—48 rnds total.

Move the last st of rnd 32 to the needle 1. This is now the first st of the rnd.

On the next rnd, work first 31 sts (the sts on ndl 1 plus the first 10 sts on ndl 2) in patt. Set these sts aside

HEEL

The heel is worked back and forth on the rem 29 sts.

Heel Flap

Work charted Heel st patt between garter st selvages for 26 rows total.

Heel Turn

Row 1 (RS): K17, ssk, k1, turn.
Row 2 (WS): Sl 1 pwise, p6, p2tog, p1, turn.
Row 3: Sl 1 kwise, knit to 1 st before gap, ssk (working 1 st before and 1 st after gap tog), k1, turn.
Row 4: Sl 1 pwise, purl to 1 st before gap, p2tog, p1, turn.
Rep Rows 3 and 4 until 17 sts rem.
K9. Place marker for beginning of rnd.

INSTEP

Return to working in the rnd and rearrange sts on Rnd 1 as foll:
Ndl 1: K8, pick up and knit 13 sts in the garter bumps along side of heel flap, M1 between ndls 1 and 2.
Ndl 2: Work patt as est.
Ndl 3: M1 between needles 2 and 3, then pick up and knit 12 sts along side of heel flap, k9.

Rnds 2 and 3: Work sole sts in St st and continue in patt on instep.
Rnd 4: K to last 3 sts on ndl 1, k2tog, k1; work patt as est on ndl 2, and on ndl 3,k1, ssk, knit to end of rnd.

Rep Rnds 3 and 4 seven times—60 sts rem.

FOOT

Work even in patts as est until 3½ repeats of Cable Patt have been worked below the ribbed cuff.

TOE

Divide sts evenly onto 4 ndls.
Work the Band Toe as follows:
Dec 1: *On ndl 1, k to last 3 sts, k2tog, k1; on ndl 2, k1, ssk, knit to end of ndl; rep from * on ndls 3 and 4.
Dec as above on the 3rd rnd twice, every other rnd 3 times, then every rnd 4 times.
On the next rnd, work k2tog with the last 2 sts on ndls 1 and 3 and ssk with the first 2 sts on ndls 2 and 4.
Divide the sts into 2 equal sections of 8 sts each and join with Kitchener st.

Make the second sock the same way.

Basics & Knitting Techniques

In this chapter you'll find the knitting basics and special techniques needed to make the projects in this book. Illustrated step-by-step instructions will clearly guide you through learning the skills you need for successful knitting.

Basic Knitting Instructions

FIRST STITCH

Pull out a tail of yarn long enough for the number of stitches you need to cast on. A good estimate is 1 in (2.5 cm) for each stitch. Hold the tail of the yarn in your left hand, and in your right hand, hold a knitting needle and the working yarn attached to the ball.

Wrap the working yarn from outside clockwise around your left thumb, so that the strands cross at the base of your thumb. Hold the tail of the yarn firmly with your left middle, ring and little fingers.

Insert the needle into the loop on your left thumb from bottom to top.

Pull out your thumb and pull the yarn so it forms the first stitch on the needle.
Do not let go of this stitch. It is not secured until the second stitch is made.

LONG TAIL CAST-ON

With the tail of the yarn over your left thumb and the yarn attached to the ball over your index finger, pull the strands open. Grasp the strands in your palm, and pull the needle down to form a "V" between your thumb and index finger.

Insert the needle into the loop on your thumb, from bottom to top. Bring the needle around the yarn on your index finger from right to left and catch the yarn on the needle. Then pull the yarn back through the loop on your thumb from top to bottom.

Pull your thumb out of the loop. You now have another stitch on the needle. Reposition your thumb under the tail, and tug gently to tighten the new stitch on the needle. Do not let go of the strands held in your palm.

Repeat until you have the required stitches on the right needle.

KNIT STITCH

Hold the needle with the stitches in your left hand and the empty needle in your right hand. With the working yarn in back of the left needle, insert the right needle under the left needle and into the first stitch from front to back, so the tip of the right needle is behind the left needle.

Wrap the working yarn around the right needle clockwise and pull the yarn through the loop on the left needle. You now have one new knit stitch on the right needle.

Drop the old stitch from the left needle. Repeat these three steps until you have the desired number of knit stitches.

Stockinette Stitch (St st)
When working back-and-forth, stockinette stitch is created by knitting every stitch on the right-side (RS) rows and purling every stitch on the wrong-side (WS) rows.

PURL STITCH

Garter Stitch
The pattern made by knitting every stitch in every row is garter stitch.

With the working yarn in front of the left needle, insert the right needle into the first stitch from back to front, so the tip of the right needle is in front of the left needle.

Wrap the working yarn around the right needle counter-clockwise and pull the yarn through. You now have one new purl stitch on the right needle.

Drop the old stitch from the left needle. Repeat these 3 steps until you have the desired number of purl stitches.

Reverse Stockinette Stitch (Rev St st)
When working back and forth, reverse stockinette stitch is created by purling every stitch on the right-side rows and knitting every stitch on the wrong-side rows.

SELVAGES (EDGE STITCHES)

The selvage or edge stitch is made by working the first and last stitch of every row in a specific manner.

Garter edge: Knit the first and last stitch of every row. This creates an edge stitch that has "beads" or "knots" on the edge of the fabric created by garter ridges.

Stockinette edge: Knit the first and last stitch of RS rows and purl the first and last stitch of WS rows. This produces a smooth edge that is easy to seam.

Slip stitch (chain) edge: Knit the first stitch of the row through the back loop and slip the last stitch purlwise with yarn held in front. This produces a "chain" edge.

All of the projects in this book are worked with edge stitches.

BRIOCHE SELVAGE

The brioche pattern requires a special selvage worked with the first and last 3 sts of the row. The selvage is similar to brioche rib, but is  worked without yarnovers. Instead, the purls are slipped with the yarn in front. The edging looks the same on RS and WS and works best with an odd number of sts.

PUTTING STITCHES ON HOLD

Sometimes you must put a portion of the stitches on hold to be worked later. When instructed to do so, you may put the stitches on a stitch holder or a piece of scrap yarn, or simply leave them unworked on a spare needle. When instructed at a later point in the pattern, these stitches may be worked separately (as in a second shoulder) or they may be rejoined with the rest of the work (such as in a sock leg or after working an armhole opening) and you return to working on all of the stitches in one row or round.

PICKING UP AND KNITTING STITCHES

Picking Up and Knitting Stitches on a Horizontal Edge

Insert the needle into the center of a stitch (into the middle of the V shape of a knit stitch) and not between 2 stitches.

Wrap the yarn around the needle and pull it to the front of the work to make a new stitch.

Picking Up and Knitting Stitches along a Vertical Edge

When you pick up and knit stitches along the selvage edge, pick up 3 stitches for every 4 rows of knitting.

CABLE CAST-ON

On some projects, you will need to cast on stitches in the middle of the piece. It is easiest to add these stitches by working a cable cast-on.

Insert the right needle between the first two stitches on the left needle from front to back. Wrap the yarn counter-clockwise and pull up a loop as if to knit. You will now have 1 new stitch on the right needle.

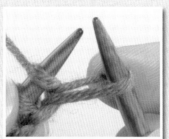

Bring the right needle up and slip the new stitch back onto the left needle. Repeat these steps until you have the desired number of new stitches.

MAKE 1 (M1)

Insert the left needle under the bar between the stitches from front to back and lift the bar onto the needle. Next, insert the right needle into the back leg of this new "stitch" from right to left and knit it. This twists the strands and creates an invisible increase.

MAKE 1 PURLWISE (M1p)

Insert the left needle under the bar between the stitches from front to back and lift the bar onto the needle. Next, insert the right needle into the back leg of this new "stitch" from right to left and purl it. This twists the strands and creates an invisible increase.

KNIT 2 TOGETHER (K2tog)

Insert the right needle into two stitches at the same time, from left to right with the right needle behind the left needle, and knit them together as one stitch.

PURL2 TOGETHER (P2tog)

Insert the right needle into two stitches at the same time, from right to left with the right needle in front of the left needle, and purl them together as one stitch.

BINDING OFF

Work 2 sts in pattern. Only these two stitches will be on the working (right) needle.

With the tip of the left needle, lift the second stitch on the right needle over the first stitch (following the arrow in the photo) and drop it off the needle—1 st bound off. Repeat across the row until the desired number of sts are bound off. At the end of the row, cut the yarn, thread the tail through the last stitch and tug gently to fasten off.

Knitting Socks

TWISTED STITCHES

K1tbl: Insert the right needle into the back leg of the next stitch from right to left and knit this stitch. The legs of the stitch will be crossed and it will be slightly tighter than a normal knit stitch.

P1tbl: Insert the right needle into the back leg of the next stitch from left to right and purl this stitch. The legs of the stitch will be crossed and it will be slightly tighter than a normal purl stitch.

Numbering the Needles
Needles are numbered from the yarn tail in the direction of knitting.

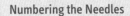

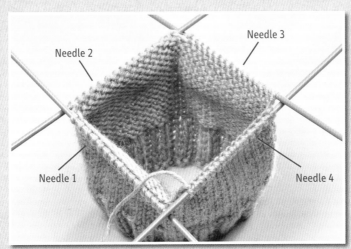

Needle 2

Needle 3

Needle 1

Needle 4

CASTING ON
After casting on, divide the stitches equally onto four (or three) double-pointed needles, as instructed. A fifth (or fourth) needle will be used for knitting. Make sure the stitches are not twisted and the cast-on edge is facing in the same direction on all of the needles. To begin knitting, work across the stitches on the needle in your left hand using an empty needle. Rotate the work and repeat from * three times. Needle 1 is the beginning of the round and needle 4 (or 3) is the end of the round. The yarn tail marks the end of the round, so no stitch marker is needed.

LEG
The sock leg is worked in the round, beginning with the cuff. Cuffs are most often worked in ribbing (for example k1, p1 or k2, p2 ribbing), because ribbing is much more elastic than stockinette and other pattern stitches.

You can work the leg in ribbing, stockinette, or another decorative pattern stitch. After the heel is worked, the foot is also worked in the round.

HEEL

The heel is worked in two parts: a rectangular flap and a turn worked with decreases to shape the curved part of the heel. The heel is followed by gusset shaping on the instep.

Heel Flap

The flap is worked back and forth on the stitches of needles 1 and 4 or on the stitches indicated in the pattern. The stitches on needles 2 and 3 are put on hold while you work the heel flap. Knit the first and last stitch of every row for a selvage that will make it easier to pick up stitches on the sides of the flap after the heel is complete. The heel is worked in St st or in the pattern stitch described in the instructions.

When the flap is the required length, work the heel turn back and forth in St st over the middle section as follows:

Heel Turn

Row 1 (RS): Knit across the indicated number of stitches, usually half of the heel stitches plus a few more, ssk, k1, turn.

Row 2 (WS): Slip 1 st purlwise, p1, purl 5 (or 6) as instructed in pattern, p2tog, p1, turn.
Row 3: Slip 1 st knitwise, k1, knit to the gap formed by the ssk on the previous RS row, ssk (working the last stitch before the gap and the first stitch after the gap together as 1 stitch), k1, turn.
Row 4: Slip 1 st purlwise, p1, purl to the gap formed by the p2tog on the previous WS row, p2tog (working the last stitch before the gap and the first stitch after the gap together as 1 stitch), p1, turn.
Repeat Rows 3 and 4 until all of the stitches have been worked and the number of stitches indicated in the pattern remain.

Picking up Stitches

Return to working in the round as follows: With needle 1, knit across the heel stitches, pick up and knit the indicated number of stitches along the side of the heel flap. Work across the instep stitches on needles 2 and 3 in pattern. With needle 4, pick up and knit the indicated number of stitches along the side of the heel flap, then knit across half of the original heel stitches. Needles 1 and 4 should each have the same number of stitches, or, if there are an odd number of stitches in the heel, needle 1 may have one more stitch. The end of the round falls between needles 1 and 4, at the center of the heel.

Instep and Gusset Shaping

After gusset sts have been picked up, the sole/gusset sts and top of foot/instep are in two separate sections. Work the sole/gusset sts in St st and continue the pattern from the leg across the top-of-foot/instep sts as follows:
Rnd 1: Knit to last 3 sole/gusset sts, k2tog, k1; work in established pattern across instep sts; on second half of sole/gusset sts, k1, ssk, knit to end of rnd.
Rnd 2: Work even in established patterns, without decreasing on the sole unless otherwise instructed.
Repeat Rnds 1 and 2 until the specified number of sts remain. Work even on the foot until it is the desired length for starting the toe.

Band Toe

For a band toe, the top of the toe is worked on needles 2 and 3, and the bottom of the toe on needles 1 and 4 with decreases made on the sides of the foot.

*On needle 1, knit to the last 3 sts, k2tog, k1. On needle 2, k1, ssk, knit to the end of the needle.

Repeat from * on needles 3 and 4.

The decreases are repeated every other round, or as indicated in the pattern, until the specified number of stitches remain on each needle. To close the toe, thread the tail of the yarn on a tapestry needle and draw it through all of the remaining stitches twice. Pull gently to gather the toe and weave in yarn tail neatly on WS of sock. If you prefer, you can join the rem sts with Kitchener st, arranging the sts on 2 needles with the sts from one side of the band on one ndl and the sts from the other side of the band on the other ndl.

Wedge Toe

For a band toe, the top of the toe is worked on needles 2 and 3, and the bottom of the toe on needles 1 and 4 with decreases made on the sides of the foot.

*On needle 1, knit to the last 3 sts, k2tog, k1. On needle 2, k1, ssk, knit to the end of the needle. Repeat from * on needles 3 and 4.

The decreases are repeated every other round, or as indi-

cated in the pattern, until 4 or 5 stitches remain on each needle as specified. Arrange the rem sts on 2 needles with the sole sts on one ndl and the sts on top of the foot on the other ndl. Close seam with Kitchener stitch.

SIZE TABLE FOR 6-PLY SOCK YARN

Sizes	22/23 Toddler 12-24 months	24/25 Toddler 2 yrs	26/27 Toddler 3 yrs	28/29 Toddler 4 yrs	30/31 Child 6 yrs	32/33 Child's 8/10 yrs/ teen small	34/35 Teen medium/ women's x-small	36/37 Teen large/ women's small	38/39 Women's medium/ men's small	40/41 Women's large/ men's medium	42/43 Women's x-large/ men's large	44/45 Men's x-large	46/47 Men's 2x
Total stitches / stitches per needle	32/8	36/9	36/9	40/10	40/10	44/11	44/11	48/12	48/12	52/13	52/13	56/14	56/14
Stitches in heel	16	18	18	20	20	22	22	24	24	26	26	28	28
Foot length to beginning of toe	12	12	13,5	14	15	16,5	17	18	20	21,5	22,5	23	24,5
Spacing of decrease rounds on toe after first decrease in 3rd round									1 x	1 x	1 x	1 x	1 x	1 x
Every other round (X times)	2 x	3 x	3 x	3 x	3 x	4 x	4 x	4 x	4 x	4 x	4 x	4 x	4 x
Every round (X times)	3 x	3 x	3 x	4 x	4 x	4 x	4 x	4 x	4 x	5 x	5 x	6 x	6 x
Total foot length	5¾ in 14,5	6 in 15,5	6¾ in 17	7 in 18	7¾ in 19,5	8¼ in 21	8¾ in 22	9¼ in 23,5	9¾ in 25	10½ in 26,5	10¾ in 27,5	11¼ in 28,5	11¾ in 30

SIZES FOR 4-PLY SOCK YARN

Sizes	22/23 Toddler 12-24 months	24/25 Toddler 2 yrs	26/27 Toddler 3 yrs	28/29 Toddler 4 yrs	30/31 Child 6 yrs	32/33 Child's 8/10 yrs/ teen small	34/35 Teen medium/ women's x-small	36/37 Teen large/ women's small	38/39 Women's medium/ men's small	40/41 Women's large/ men's medium	42/43 Women's x-large/ men's large	44/45 Men's x-large	46/47 Men's 2x
Total stitches / stitches per needle	44/11	48/12	48/12	52/13	52/13	56/14	56/14	60/15	60/15	64/16	64/16	68/17	72/18
Stitches in heel	22	24	24	26	26	28	28	30	30	32	32	34	36
Foot length to beginning of toe	11,5	12,5	14	14	15,5	17	18	18,5	20	21	22	22,5	24
Spacing of decrease rounds on toe after first decrease in 3rd round									1 x	1 x	1 x	1 x	1 x	1 x
Every 3rd round (X times)	1 x	1 x	1 x	2 x	2 x	2 x	2 x	2 x	2 x	2 x	2 x	2 x	2 x
Every other round (X times)	3 x	3 x	3 x	3 x	3 x	3 x	3 x	3 x	3 x	3 x	3 x	4 x	4 x
Every round (X times)	4 x	5 x	5 x	5 x	5 x	6 x	6 x	6 x	6 x	7 x	7 x	7 x	8 x
Total foot length	5¾ in 14,5	6 in 15,5	6¾ in 17	7 in 18	7¾ in 19,5	8¼ in 21	8¾ in 22	9¼ in 23,5	9¾ in 25	10½ in 26,5	10¾ in 27,5	11¼ in 28,5	11¾ in 30

Miscellaneous Techniques

MATTRESS STITCH

Mattress stitch is the most commonly used method of seaming knitted pieces.

With the right sides facing up, place the two pieces to be seamed on a flat surface.

With a tapestry needle and matching yarn, go under the bar between first and second stitches near the edge of one piece of knitting. Repeat on the other piece. For a quicker seam, catch two bars from each side as you make each stitch. Continue to work from side to side, pulling gently on the yarn to close the seam every 2 in (5 cm).

KITCHENER STITCH

1. (Set-up) Hold the two pieces together on the two knitting needles, wrong sides together, positioned so the working strand comes from the right-hand stitch on the front needle. Insert the tapestry needle into the first stitch on the back needle as if to knit, but don't take the stitch off its needle. Now insert the tapestry needle into the first stitch on the front needle as if to purl, and again don't take the stitch off the needle.

2. (Back needle) Take the tapestry needle to the back needle and insert it in the first stitch as if to purl and remove that stitch from its needle. Insert the tapestry needle into the next stitch as if to knit but do not remove it.

3. (Front needle) Take the tapestry needle to the front needle and insert it in the first stitch as if to knit and remove that stitch from its needle. Insert the tapestry needle into the next stitch as if to purl but do not remove it. Repeat steps 2 and 3 until one stitch remains on each needle. Follow the established pattern as well as possible with these two stitches. One st will be removed from its needle after the second pass of the tapestry needle; there will be no second stitch on that needle to go through before moving to the other needle. The final stitch will only be entered once with the tapestry needle. Fasten off.

END-TO-END SEAM

End-to-end seams are used to join the cast-on and bound-off edges of knit pieces.

With the right sides of the fabric facing up, place the two pieces to be seamed on a flat surface. With a tapestry needle and matching yarn, catch the knit V just inside the edge of one piece of knitting. Repeat on the other piece.

Continue to work from side to side, pulling gently on the yarn to close the seam after each stitch. The seam should be at the same tension as your knitting, and look like a row of stockinette stitch.

GAUGE

Gauge is a measurement of how tight your knitting is. It is measured in stitches per inch or cm (width) and rows per inch or cm (height). To insure your garments come out the right size, you need to make a gauge swatch. To measure your gauge, knit a swatch that is at least 6 in / 15 cm square in the pattern stitch indicated in the project.

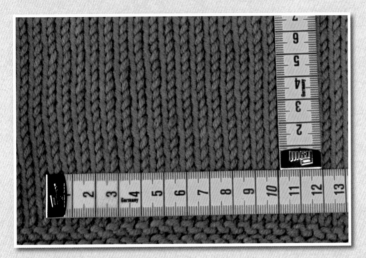

If your gauge is not exact, your garment will not come out the width indicated in the pattern. To measure the stitch gauge, place a ruler or tape measure across your swatch horizontally. Mark the beginning and end of 4 in / 10 cm and count the stitches.
To measure the row gauge, place a ruler or tape measure across your swatch vertically. Mark the beginning and end of 4 in / 10 cm and count the rows.

If the number of stitches and rows in your swatch is:
more than recommended, try again with a smaller needle;
fewer than recommended, try a larger needle.

READING CHARTS

A chart is a picture of the stitch pattern that is made using special symbols for pattern stitches. Each square in the chart represents one stitch. Blank squares appear in some of the charts as placeholders where stitches have been removed (by decreasing) or will be added (by increasing). This symbol is referred to as "no stitch" in chart keys. You just skip over these blank squares when knitting. They are there only to help align the other symbols in the chart so you can more easily visualize what the knitted pattern will look like.

Charts help you see what the pattern motif will look like before you begin knitting, so, a chart is easier to follow than line-by-line written instructions. Because knitting chart symbols are not standardized around the world, each symbol is defined on the same page as the chart using that symbol.
To read a chart, start at the bottom for Row 1.

If you are knitting back-and-forth:
RS rows are read from right to left.
WS rows are read from left to right (because you turn your knitting and go back in the opposite direction to work the WS rows).

If you are knitting in the round, all rows are read from right to left (because you never turn your work and all rounds are completed by knitting in the same direction).

The numbers on the right side of the chart represent the rows or rounds of knitting. If there are only odd numbers, the wrong-side or even-numbered rows are not shown. Check the instructions to find out how to knit the wrong-side rows. Generally, you will knit the stitches as they appear. That is, you will knit the knits and purl the purls as they face you.

The pattern repeat is marked on the chart. Sometimes the entire chart is repeated across a row, and sometimes there are special stitches that are worked at the beginning or end of the row that are not repeated. In this case, you begin by working the stitch(es) before the marked repeat section of the chart once, then work the repeat section over and over again until the last stitch(es) of the row, and end by working the final stitch(es) of the chart once. You may also have selvage stitches that are worked at the beginning and end of the row. In this case, you may find that placing a marker inside the edge stitches helps you more easily keep track.

The row repeat may be all of the rows in the chart, or there may be setup rows that are worked only once at the beginning of the pattern. This will be indicated in the project instructions.

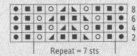

● = Selvage stitch for a stockinette edge: knit on RS and purl on WS

■ = Knit

○ = Yarn over

◢ = Purl

◤ = K2tog

In color charts, each square also represents a stitch and the color of the square indicates the color of yarn to use for that stitch.

BLOCKING AND SHAPING PIECES

To block your pieces, cut out actual size pieces with white paper, following the outline of the schematic drawing. Baker's paper or tissue paper are also good choices. Newspaper is not suitable because the ink may rub off on your knitting.

Wash your pieces, shape them on the paper pattern, and dry flat.

Note The paper pattern can also help you keep track of your knitting. As you knit each piece, put the paper pattern on a bulletin board, the wall, or your refrigerator and hold your knitting up to it to see when you have reached the desired length. If you make any changes as you go, you can also make notes on the paper pattern.

FRINGE

A basic fringe is made by adding strands of yarn evenly spread out across the ends of a piece. Cut 2 to 4 strands of yarn twice the length of the finished fringe and fold in half. You can wrap the yarn around a piece of cardboard to make it easier to cut the strands a consistent length. Insert a crochet hook through a stitch on the edge of the piece and draw through a loop from

the center of the folded fringe. Draw the ends of the fringe strands through the folded loop and tug gently on the ends to secure. If desired, trim fringes, knot them to form a decorative pattern, or add beads. To avoid splitting the ends of the fringe, you can tie a knot at the end of each strand after trimming the fringe.

CROCHET EDGINGS

Single Crochet (sc)

Single Crochet makes a smooth edge that looks like the bind-off edge of knitting. On cast-on and bind-off edges, work 1 sc in each knit st. When crocheting along with sides of a knitted piece, work 3 sc for every 4 rows.

Insert a crochet hook into a stitch on the edge of the knitting, and draw a loop through to the front. Wrap the yarn around the hook and draw a second loop through the first to secure. *Working from right to left, insert the crochet hook into the next stitch on the edge of the piece. Pull the working yarn through to the front. Two loops are now on the hook. Pull the working yarn through both loops on the hook. One loop remains on the hook. Repeat from * until the entire edge is covered. If working in the round, slip stitch to the first stitch of the round to join.

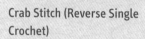

Picots

In the second row or round, you can add picots for a decorative effect:

Irish Picots: *Work 3 single crochet, chain 4, work 1 single crochet in the next stitch; rep from *.

Picot Shells: *Work 1 single crochet, chain 4, slip st into the top of the single crochet, work 2 single crochet.

Crab Stitch (Reverse Single Crochet)

Crab Stitch – also known as reverse single crochet because it is worked in the opposite direction – creates a decorative beaded edge. Crab stitch can be worked as an edging on its own, or after a row of single crochet.

Insert a crochet hook into a stitch on the edge of the piece, and draw a loop through to the

front. Wrap the yarn around the hook and draw a second loop through the first to secure. *Working from left to right, insert the crochet hook into the next stitch on the edge of the piece of knitting. Pull the working yarn through to the front giving the hook a twist as you pull it through so the two loops cross. Be careful not to pull it through the loop already on the hook. Two loops are now on the hook, but they cross each other. Pull the working yarn through both loops on the hook. One loop remains on the hook. Repeat from * until the entire edge is covered. If working in the round, slip stitch to the first stitch of the round to join.

ABBREVIATIONS

approx	approximately
BO	bind off
cn	cable needle
CO	cast on
cont	continue
dec(s)	decrease(s)(ing)
dpn(s)	double pointed needle(s)
est	established
foll	follow(s)(ing)
g	grams
inc(s)	increase(s)(ing)
k	knit
k2tog	knit 2 sts together
kwise	knitwise (or as if to knit)
M1	make 1
M1p	make 1 purlwise
meas	Measures
m	meters
ndl(s)	needle(s)
p	purl
p2tog	purl 2 sts together
patts	pattern(s)
pm	place marker
pwise	purlwise (or as if to purl)
rem	remain(s)(ing)
rep	repeat
rnd(s)	round(s)
RS	right side
sl	slip
sl1-k1-psso	Slip 1 k1, knit 1, pass the slipped-st over
sl2-k1-p2sso	slip 2 sts tog k2 as if to k2tog, knit 1, pass the 2 slipped sts over
ssk	(Slip 1 knitwise) twice, insert left needle into front of the 2 sts just slipped and knit them tog through the back
st(s)	stitch(es)
tog	together
WS	wrong side
wyib	with yarn in back
wyif	with yarn in front
yd	yards

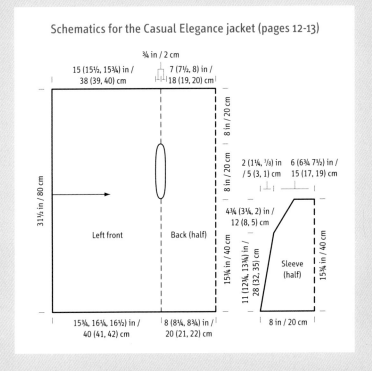

Schematics for the Casual Elegance jacket (pages 12-13)

For information on selecting or substituting yarn contact your local yarn shop or an online store, they are familiar with all types of yarns and would be happy to help you. Additionally, the online knitting community at Ravelry.com has forums where you can post questions about specific yarns. Yarns come and go so quickly these days and there are so many beautiful yarns available.